Tom Bandy's Church Transformation Trilogy provides a comprehensive resource to envision, reflect, and implement a thriving church that can grow in spiritual depth and mission outreach. Each book reinforces, and builds upon, the others. Start with any of the three books, and follow the flow of transformation in your unique context.

Facing Reality is the congregational mission assessment tool that enables church leaders to examine congregational life honestly and thoroughly, and point the congregation beyond itself toward mission in the postmodern world.

Go to *Kicking Habits: Upgrade Edition* for a large overview of systemic change, and to see the vision of thriving church life that lies behind the data collection and interpretation of *Facing Reality.* This book interprets the attitude shift that is implied by all the strategic change, and answers the question "Where will all this research lead?"

Go to *Coming Clean* for a practical study guide that helps you reflect on the stories of systemic change and apply the strategies of simultaneous de-construction and re-construction for your context. This book will answer the question "How can we adapt and interpret the research for our context?"

Return to *Facing Reality* better equipped to discern your congregation's place in the continuum of addiction and health using the classic *7 Deadly Sins* and *7 Lively Virtues.*

FACING REALITY

A CONGREGATIONAL MISSION ASSESSMENT TOOL

THOMAS G. BANDY

ABINGDON PRESS/Nashville

FACING REALITY: A CONGREGATIONAL MISSION ASSESSMENT TOOL

This book is printed on acid-free paper.

Library of Congress Cataloging-in-Publication Data

Bandy, Thomas G., 1950–
Facing reality: a congregational mission assessment tool: a tool for systematic change and church transformation / Thomas G. Bandy.
p. cm.
ISBN 0-687-09808-4 (alk. paper)
1. Church renewal—Handbooks, manuals, etc. 2. Church growth—Handbooks, manuals, etc. I. Title.

BV600.3 .B36 2001
250—dc21 00-065038

01 02 03 04 05 06 07 08 09 10—10 9 8 7 6 5 4 3 2 1

MANUFACTURED IN THE UNITED STATES OF AMERICA

CONTENTS

INTRODUCTION

Can a declining traditional church transform itself to thrive in the twenty-first century? This question has occupied my ministry throughout my career as a pastor, denominational leader, and consultant. The answer is yes—provided that the congregation is willing to undertake a transformation of the entire flow of congregational life.

The challenge of the twenty-first century is that mere church renewal will not revitalize a congregation anymore. No single program, curriculum, staffing change, outreach mission, or creative idea will be enough to leverage sufficient change in the church necessary to address the needs of the post-modern world. It is the system of congregational life itself that must be redesigned.

This insight led me to profile the declining and thriving church systems in my book *Kicking Habits: Welcome Relief for Addicted Churches*. I demonstrated that the root cause of church decline or growth has everything to do with the holistic health of the congregation and less to do with any particular piece of a strategic plan. In order to grow, churches must not only discern their strengths and weaknesses, but they must overcome addictive behavior patterns that permeate all aspects of congregational life and mission. Systemic addiction will sabotage the best strategic plans, cripple the best creative ideas, and undermine the best leaders. Systemic health will allow a congregation to seize emerging opportunities quickly, make the most of its limited resources, and empower even the most timid leaders.

Over the years, I have refined the congregational consultation tool that I first presented in my book *Moving Off the Map: A Field Guide to Changing Your Congregation*. The tool has become shorter but more powerful. It has been joined with other support tools to help even the smallest congregation discover a healthier future. Since systemic change is so stressful for both congregations and congregational leaders, I have added extra tools to discern leadership readiness in order to predict the reasonable pace of change. The faster a church transforms itself, the more stressful it will be for members and leaders. *Many congregations today, however, do not have much time left!*

I encourage you to read carefully the two books that provide direct background to *Facing Reality: Kicking Habits: Welcome Relief for Addicted Churches* and *Moving Off the Map: A Field Guide to Changing Your Congregation*. Both books are available through Abingdon Press or Cokesbury or at www.easumband.com, which is the *Easum, Bandy, & Associates* Web site.

You will quickly realize that *Facing Reality* is not a small undertaking. It will take significant time and energy, and it will bring both stress and excitement to the congregation. The question you are probably asking is, *Why should we do it? Why should we spend so much energy on something that may well disturb our contentment and place new demands on our leadership?*

There really is only one answer. You will only do this if you want to be with Jesus Christ in the mission field of today. If your goal is only to preserve a heritage, take care of church insiders, or survive as a community institution, the congregational mission assessment tool is not for you. However, if you want to be where Jesus is, help others experience the Holy, and pass on the pearl of greatest worth in your life to countless people hungering for hope, then it will be worth all the effort and stress to reorient your congregational life. In the end, only the gospel matters. Everything else is tactics.

Tom Bandy
January, 2000

GENERAL INSTRUCTIONS

Facing Reality contains a variety of tools to collect information and perspectives about your congregation and congregational leadership. This will require time and effort. The worksheets can be completed in about four weeks, but this depends upon the current state of church records, the size and energy of the planning team, and the attention of the staff and official body. Many congregations allow about three months to gather all the information. It usually takes another month for a consultant or congregational leaders to digest and interpret the information. At the end of this process, there may be an additional on-site consultation providing time for personal conversations that go deeper into particular issues. A final report that includes recommendations for the future can then be completed.

You will need a planning team to coordinate research and collate information. This team may be composed of five to seven people, and they may need additional help for specific tasks. This planning team should include people with skills in gathering information and enthusiasm for the process. It is most helpful if they also have communication skills to articulate the purpose of the process and encourage participation.

There is no blueprint explaining how to proceed in the process, but you may wish to follow these steps:

a) Review all the tools to become familiar with the information required and the sources from which the information or perspectives will be gathered. Discern the current state of church records about the congregation and surrounding community and identify key gaps in knowledge that you will need to address.

b) Read *Kicking Habits: Welcome Relief for Addicted Churches* and *Moving Off the Map: A Field Guide for Changing Your Congregation* (both published by Abingdon Press).

c) Use *Coming Clean: A Study Guide for Kicking Habits* to build congregational understanding for change and to introduce *Facing Reality*.

d) Widely publicize the process in the church, and explain the motivation behind it during worship services.

e) Gather demographic information. If necessary, distribute the survey tool entitled "A Profile of Our Congregation" to gain demographic information that you lack about the membership. You may wish to use national or municipal census information, data from a local business association, or information from independent companies, like Percept in the United States, to gain these demographics.

f) Distribute the worksheets found in *Facing Reality* for the staff and official body, respectively, to complete.

g) Distribute the "Church Stress Test" in connection with any two consecutive worship services, and combine the returned answers on a single summary sheet. You can use the test during, or immediately after, the worship service.

h) Mail the "Random Congregational Survey" to members and regular adherents of the church.

i) Distribute the "Worship Service Survey" at least once for each worship service you celebrate, and combine the returns on a single summary sheet. You can use the worship survey within, or following, the worship service.

j) Distribute the "Leadership Readiness Test" to the staff and official body. While each person may complete the test, an average score needs to be provided.

k) As completed worksheets are returned, collate and summarize the results on the assessment tool's summary worksheet.

l) Send the summary sheet to the consultant (if a consultant is involved), but keep the other individual worksheets in safekeeping in case the consultant needs to refer to them to clarify some point. For example, it is sometimes helpful to examine the responses from each worship service separately to discover if one congregation has very different perspectives from another or to examine the individual responses to the "Leadership Readiness Test" to discover if some leaders have a different perspective from other leaders.

m) If you are interpreting the results without a consultant, use the "Ancient Diagnosis for Today's Congregation" to help you discern positive or negative patterns in the church. The assessment tool's master summary worksheet is coded to help you focus on key questions; these codes are explained in "Ancient Diagnosis for Today's Congregation."

n) If you are interpreting the results without a consultant, share the master summary worksheet and the "Ancient Diagnosis for Today's Congregation" with partner congregational or judicatory leaders and invite their objective comment.

You will find more specific instructions with each tool. You will undoubtedly need to customize the process to your particular context. Just remember that our goal is to gather accurate information, listen to perspectives from a wide spectrum of church participants and leaders, and discern opportunities, obstacles, and patterns that your congregation will need to address.

The more carefully and accurately you work, the more specific and helpful future interpretations and recommendations will be. Only do the process for congregational mission assessment in the context of continuous prayerful support by the entire congregation. The assessment process and the future of the church should be the priority focus of prayer, Bible study, reflection, and conversation throughout the time of the research.

THE COMPLETE CONGREGATIONAL MISSION ASSESSMENT

Facing Reality asks 10 key questions in each of the eleven subsystems of congregational life. These sub-systems are explained in greater detail in the book *Moving Off the Map: A Field Guide to Changing Your Congregation* by Tom Bandy (Abingdon Press). **Note:** To facilitate the assessment tool's use in survey and consultation, some of the section headings have been articulated more concretely here. The eleven subsystems are:

Foundational:	Genetic Code	*The identity of the church*
	Core Leadership	*The seriousness for mission in the church*
	Organization	*The structure of the church*
Functional:	Changing People	*How people experience God in the church*
	Growing Christians	*How people grow in relationship to Jesus*
	Discerning Call	*How people discover their place in God's plan*
	Equipping Disciples	*How people are trained for ministries*
	Deploying Servants	*How people are sent into the world and supported by the church*
Formal:	Property	*Location, facility, and technology*
	Finance	*Stewardship, budget, and debt-management*
	Communication	*Information, marketing, and advertising*

The questions in each subsystem have been coded to allow the consultant to observe chains of positive habits or destructive addictions that influence the success or failure of strategic plans. The code for each question identifies the question with one of the addiction-health polarities on the next page. The middle column indicates which questions pertain to which addiction-health polarity. This allows you to focus on a particular set of questions to determine the degree of addiction or health that is experienced by that church. This is not a quantifiable science. It is an art. Study the definitions of the sins and virtues on the next page and anticipate how you might "score" your church on a scale of 1 (deeply addicted) to 10 (extremely healthy). Later, when your research is complete, ask several church leaders to do this also and compare your results. If a professional church consultant has interpreted the assessment tool, compare his or her assessment as well. (See the last chapter, "An Ancient Diagnosis for Today's Congregation," for a complete discussion.)

The Seven Deadly Sins		The Seven Cardinal Virtues
1. PRIDE The elevation of the church to ultimacy. Institutional arrogance. Self-centeredness that expects the world to accommodate itself to the forms, habits, and expectations of institutional religion. It is the belief that the world revolves around the church, must wait for the church, and is ultimately judged by the church. It is the egotistical conviction that the mission field can be addressed at the convenience of the church.	**PF Questions** 1, 2, 3, 4, 7, 12, 15, 22, 23, 30, 31, 32, 37, 38, 49, 52, 53, 57, 77, 84, 90, 92, 102, 104, 109, 110	**1. FAITH** The surrender of the church to the ultimacy of Christ. Institutional humility. The compassionate prioritizing of strategies that lead the church to adapt itself to the cultural forms of real people. It is the urgency to engage in mission now, before it is too late, and before God judges the church for failing to rescue the lost. It is the selfless conviction that the mission of the church is more important than the survival of an institutional franchise.
2. COVETOUSNESS The institutional desire to possess what is not theirs. An obsession with material wealth. The elevation of "things" to a core value. It is the preoccupation of the church with property and money and the desire to acquire the wealth of others to perpetuate institutional comfort. It is the habitual reduction of programs to balance the budget, obsession with debt freedom, and the expectation that society should spend itself for the sake of denominational heritage.	**CC Questions** 1, 7, 8, 27, 28, 33, 38, 44, 64, 66, 67, 70, 71, 73, 74, 75, 78, 83, 85, 86, 91, 92, 95, 97, 100, 101, 106, 107, 110	**2. CHARITY** The institutional audacity to give away life. The acquisition of wealth for the sole purpose of maximizing mission. The motivation to walk a second mile, endure abuse, and give away the best. The habitual, positive preference to *give* a break rather than *get* a tax break. It is the recognition by the church that stewardship embraces everything and there is no separation between sacred and secular. It is the readiness to risk property, modify plans, and change agendas to seize moments to bless others.
3. LUST Abuse of others as a means to personal or corporate satisfaction. An absolute desire to control others completely. It is the passion to possess the life of another, or make another dependent upon the organization or its leaders. It is *eros* disguised as *agape*, or ego camouflaged as pastoral care. It is the demand to be praised, loved, and cared for.	**LP Questions** 9, 13, 14, 17, 19, 21, 22, 23, 39, 40, 43, 54, 61, 63, 69, 70, 76, 77, 81, 82, 83, 85, 86, 87, 91, 92, 98, 99, 103, 105, 108, 110	**3. PRUDENCE** Respect for another's intrinsic autonomy and worth. Wisdom that limits self-satisfaction for the sake of another. Responsible freedom. It is the readiness to give permission to act independently and discover self-fulfillment beyond institutional commitments. It is the true unity of *eros* and *agape*, or the balance of self-sacrifice and self-affirmation.
4. ENVY The desire to be other than what God created the organization to be. Self-rejection. The refusal to acknowledge one's own mission potential and the jealous imitation of another organization's lifestyle. It is blaming other powers for organizational failure. It is habitual lamentation that "If only someone or something were different, we would be all right."	**EH Questions** 1, 5, 6, 27, 28, 33, 36, 38, 41, 44, 50, 52, 57, 58, 73, 78, 80, 92, 93, 94, 96, 102, 104, 109, 110	**4. HOPE** The desire to become whatever God wills. Self-acceptance. The conviction that God's power will bear fruit, and that the church can overcome all obstacles when it is true to its unique calling. It is taking ownership of failure and intentionally learning from inevitable mistakes. It is the habitual celebration and belief that "if we hold Jesus' hand, we can walk on water."
5. GLUTTONY Consumption. Excess, Self-aggrandizement. It is the desire to bring people in, rather than send people out. It is preoccupation with how newcomers can serve the institution rather than serve God. It is valuing size over quality, accountability over productivity, and process over results. It is the willingness to waste energy in pointless pursuits.	**GT Questions** 11, 12, 16, 19, 20, 23, 24, 25, 29, 31, 34, 35, 40, 48, 49, 54, 60, 65, 68, 71, 81, 92, 93, 94, 96, 97, 108, 110	**5. TEMPERANCE** Moderation. Reasonable limitation. Self-control. It is the desire to bring people into church so they can more effectively live beyond the church. It is the appropriate fulfillment of needs, building up of character, and training of relevant skills. It is valuing excellence over mediocrity, trust over control. It is the willingness to spend everything for a truly greater good.
6. ANGER The desire to harm or hurt. Physical, emotional, relational, or spiritual violence. It is the habitual, negative preference to kill, repulse, or limit the good within others. It is sardonic pleasure in justice, and twisted joy in retribution. It is misrepresenting prophetic leadership by taking delight in breaking relationships, splitting organizations, or humiliating adversaries.	**AJ Questions** 1, 5, 6, 26, 38, 39, 45, 50, 55, 64, 66, 67, 71, 75, 78, 79, 92, 95, 98, 99, 101, 106, 107, 110	**6. JUSTICE** The desire to vindicate and redeem. Physical, emotional, relational, or spiritual healing. It is principled counteraction against violent people. It is redemptive punishment for the goal of reconciliation. It is unbearable restlessness in the face of inequality, bigotry, or cultural insensitivity. It is visionary leadership that delights in synthesizing "both-and" situations. It is the difference between victory and peace.
7. SLOTH Laziness. Lack of discipline. It is the expectation that others (staff or volunteers) will do your work for you. It is the profound unwillingness to grow personally, spiritually, or professionally. It is the easy readiness to give up. It is the despairing conviction of organizational impotence that paralyzes action.	**SF Questions** 8, 10, 13, 14, 18, 23, 24, 25, 30, 32, 33, 34, 35, 42, 45, 46, 47, 48, 51, 53, 56, 59, 60, 62, 68, 72, 80, 88, 89, 92, 101, 110	**7. FORTITUDE** Energy. Discipline. It is the ability to do whatever it takes to discern, address, and accomplish one's own work. It is a passion to grow in every way. It is dogged persistence to try every means to accomplish goals. It is courageous confidence to tap hidden resources in order to take mission risks.

In addition to the assessment form itself, the congregation must complete and provide three other pieces of research:

1. Community demographic data
2. "The Leadership Readiness Test": completed by the staff and official body
3. "The Church Stress Test": completed by the worshiping congregation, staff, and official body

These are included in the package of consulting tools presented to you.

Finally, in order to complete the assessment form, you will find it helpful to use the enclosed worksheets. Some of the questions require factual information to answer. Other questions seek personal opinions or perspectives. Worksheets provided are to be used by specific groups of people in the church. The responses to the worksheets can then be summarized and recorded on the master assessment form. All the worksheets and forms can be found both in print and on CD-ROM. *If you are working with a consultant, be sure to provide the summary both in print and on computer disk. Be sure to keep the individual worksheets as well in case they are needed for further investigation.*

The Congregational Mission Assessment process
requires significant, designated time and energy to complete.
The more carefully you work now,
the more helpful the recommendations
for future planning and change will be later.

If the process includes an on-site visit with the consultant, important additional insight can be gained. The consultant should provide a preliminary report at the time of the visit and send a final written report to the congregation shortly thereafter. You may wish to share the results with congregational or judicatory colleagues for their perspective and arrange for additional coaching in the months ahead.

MASTER SUMMARY WORKSHEET

Each question indicates the worksheet or resource where the data or responses have been collected.

Foundation

Genetic Code:

1. What are the age, marital status, race or cultural origin, and educational level of adult worshipers? **Staff Worksheet, Worship Worksheet** (PF, CC, EH, AJ)

Birth Years

Line		1966–1985 % of congregation	1946–1965 % of congregation	1936–1945 % of congregation	1915–1935 % of congregation	1900–1914 % of congregation
1	Total % in this age group					

Demographic Diversity

Line		% of adult worshipers		Line		% of adult worshipers
				7	**Household Income:** Under $10,000	
1	**Married**				$10,000–29,999	
2	**Divorced/Separated**				$30,000–49,999	
3	**Widowed**				$50,000–69,999	
4	**Never married**				$70,000–89,999	
					Over $90,000	
5	**Households with children at home**					
				8	**Homeowners**	
				9	**Renters**	
6	**Cultural Background:** Western European				**Education:** Below high school	
	Eastern European				High school	
	African				College/University	
	Hispanic				Career training	
	Caribbean				Advanced degree	
	Asian					
	Pacific Rim			10	**Technology Use:**	
	Middle Eastern				Cell phone	
	Far Eastern				Computer	
	Native North				Internet	
	American				Microwave	

How does this compare with demographic statistics for the area? **Demographic Research, Staff Worksheet** (PF, CC, EH, AJ)

Birth Years

Line		1966–1985 % of population	1946–1965 % of population	1936–1945 % of population	1915–1935 % of population	1900–1914 % of population
	Total % in this age group					

Demographic Diversity

Line		% of adult population		Line		% of adult population
				7	**Household Income:** Under $10,000	
1	**Married**				$10,000–29,999	
2	**Divorced/Separated**				$30,000–49,999	
3	**Widowed**				$50,000–69,999	
4	**Never married**				$70,000–89,999	
					Over $90,000	
5	**Households with children at home**					
				8	**Homeowners**	
				9	**Renters**	
6	**Cultural Background:** Western European				**Education:** Below high school	
	Eastern European				High school	
	African				College/University	
	Hispanic				Career training	
	Caribbean				Advanced degree	
	Asian					
	Pacific Rim			10	**Technology Use:**	
	Middle Eastern				Cell phone	
	Far Eastern				Computer	
	Native North American				Internet	
					Microwave	

2. How do people start attending this church? (**Note:** Calculate percentage of respondents) **Worship Worksheet, Random Survey** (PF)

- As a result of a particular mission or ministry of the church ___
- As a result of an invitation from a member ___
- By choosing this church out of several visited ___
- By growing up in this church ___

3. What are the media preferences of the congregation? (**Note:** Calculate percentage of choices against total respondents) **Worship Worksheet, Random Survey** (PF)

Radio:	Country	___	Soft Rock	___	Classical	___
	Christian	___	Hard Rock	___	News/Talk	___
	"Oldies"	___	Rap	___	Public Radio	___
Television:	Daytime Soaps	___	Game Shows	___	Movie: Comedy	___
	Daytime Reruns	___	Sports	___	Movie: Drama	___
	Sitcoms	___	News	___	Movie: Action	___
	Talk Shows	___	Educational	___	Other	___
	List favorite television shows: ______________________					
Magazine:	Current Events	___	Transportation	___	Sports	___
	Special Interest	___	Educational	___	Home and Garden	___
	List favorite magazine______________________					

4. How welcome and included do people feel in this church? (**Note:** Calculate percentage of choices against total respondents for each point on the continuum) **Worship Worksheet, Random Survey** (PF)

I still feel like an outsider!	**1**	**2**	**3**	**4**	**5**	**6**	**7**	**8**	**9**	**10**	**They took me right into their hearts!**
% of respondents											

5. What are the core values of the congregation? **Staff Worksheet, Official Body Worksheet** (AJ, EH) A *core value* is the positive preference or choice congregational participants make, both habitually and daringly, in daily living. See *Moving Off the Map* for detailed descriptions.

Staff Perspective:	*Official Body Perspective:*
1.	1.
2.	2.
3.	3.
4.	4.
5.	5.

6. What are the bedrock beliefs of the congregation? **Staff Worksheet, Official Body Worksheet** (AJ, EH) A *bedrock belief* is the principle, symbol, or faith story that congregational participants return to for strength in times of confusion or stress. See *Moving Off the Map* for detailed descriptions.

Staff Perspective:	*Official Body Perspective:*
1.	1.
2.	2.
3.	3.
4.	4.
5.	5.

7. What is the motivating vision of the congregation? **Staff Worksheet, Official Body Worksheet** (PF, CC) A *motivating vision* is the song, image, picture, or symbol, the mere recollection of which elicits joy, shapes personal lifestyle, and demands to be shared with strangers. See *Moving Off the Map* for detailed descriptions.

   Staff perspective:

   Official body perspective:

8. What is the key mission of the congregation? **Staff Worksheet, Official Body Worksheet** (SF, CC) A *key mission* is everything that needs to be said about the church to invite enormous congregational courage and excite the imagination of the public—and can be printed on the side of a city bus. See *Moving Off the Map* for detailed descriptions.

   Staff perspective:

   Official body perspective:

9. How is the genetic code of identity (values, beliefs, vision, mission) embedded in every new member, leader, program, alternate worship service, and ministry of the congregation? **Staff Worksheet** (LP)

	Tactics	Resources
Each new member:		
Each leader:		
Each program:		
Each worship service:		
Each ministry:		

10. How is the genetic code of identity (values, beliefs, vision, mission) communicated beyond the church? **Staff Worksheet** (SF)

	Tactics	Resources
To the general public:		
To the social service sector:		
To the government sector:		
To the business sector:		
To the education sector:		

Core Leadership:

11. Identify all salaried staff (part- and full-time, honorarium or full benefits). **Official Body Worksheet** (GT)

Position	Part- or Full-time	Honorarium or Benefits	Current Salary

12. In the perspectives of others, does the pastor model the values, beliefs, vision, and mission of the congregation? **Staff, Official Body, and Worship Worksheets, Random Survey** (PF, GT) (**Note:** Record the average score from each worksheet on a 1-10 scale with 1 being an outright "no" and 10 being a wholehearted "yes.")

    Staff perspective: ___
    Official body perspective: ___
    Worshipers perspective: ___
    Random survey: ___

13. In the perspectives of others, does the official body of elected officers model the values, beliefs, vision, and mission of the congregation? **Staff, Official Body, and Worship Worksheets** (SF, LP) (**Note:** Record the average score from each worksheet on a 1-10 scale with 1 being an outright "no" and 10 being a wholehearted "yes.")

    Staff perspective: ___
    Official body perspective: ___
    Worshipers perspective: ___

14. In the perspectives of others, do the core leaders of group, program, or ministry volunteers model the values, beliefs, vision, and mission of the congregation? **Staff, Official Body, and Worship Worksheets, Random Survey** (SF, LP) (**Note:** Record the average score from each worksheet on a 1-10 scale with 1 being an outright "no" and 10 being a wholehearted "yes.")

    Staff perspective: ___
    Official body perspective: ___
    Worshipers perspective: ___
    Random survey: ___

15. How does the pastor invest his or her time and energy? **Staff, Official Body, and Worship Worksheets** (PF) (**Note:** Record the average percentages from each column of each worksheet. Do a separate report for each associate or team "pastor." The total of each perspective should equal 100 percent.)

PASTOR(S)	**Position Title:**	**% of energy on church members**	**% of energy on non-members**	**% of energy on personal growth**	**% of energy on denominational duties**	**% of energy on other personal and family issues**
Staff perspective						
Official body perspective						
Worshipers perspective						

16. How do core leaders who work in each of the following program areas invest their time and energy? **Staff, Official Body, and Worship Worksheets** (GT) (**Note:** Record the *average percentages* from each column of each worksheet. Do a separate report for each staff position, such as organist, choir director, drama coordinator, Christian education director, youth minister, counselor, pastoral visitor, and so on. The total of each perspective should equal 100 percent.)

WORSHIP PROGRAM	**Position Title:**	**% of energy on church members**	**% of energy on non-members**	**% of energy on personal growth**	**% of energy on denominational duties**	**% of energy on other personal and family issues**
Staff perspective						
Official body perspective						
Worshipers perspective						

EDUCATION PROGRAM	**Position Title:**	**% of energy on church members**	**% of energy on non-members**	**% of energy on personal growth**	**% of energy on denominational duties**	**% of energy on other personal and family issues**
Staff perspective						
Official body perspective						
Worshipers perspective						

VISITATION PROGRAM	**Position Title:**	**% of energy on church members**	**% of energy on non-members**	**% of energy on personal growth**	**% of energy on denominational duties**	**% of energy on other personal and family issues**
Staff perspective						
Official body perspective						
Worshipers perspective						

17. Rank, in order of importance, how the congregation discovers and appoints volunteers. **Official Body Worksheet** (LP)

Nominations processes	___	Time/Talent inventories	___
Formal interviews	___	Gifts discernment inventories	___
Appointments	___	Personality inventories	___
Appeals to fill vacancies	___	Call discernment processes	___

Other ____

18. How does the congregation train and equip church leaders? **Official Body Worksheet** (SF)

Position or Program	Is initial training required?	Average initial training time	Is follow-up training required?	Average follow-up training time	Who does the training?	Budget for training
Pastor						Training budget for staff:
Program staff						
Support staff						
Worship area volunteers						Training budget for volunteers:
Education area volunteers						
Visitation area volunteers						
Outreach area volunteers						

19. What methods and resources are used in training church leaders? **Official Body Worksheet** (LP, GT)

Position or Program	What resources are used?	What teaching methods are used?
Pastor		
Program staff		
Support staff		
Worship area volunteers		
Education area volunteers		
Visitation area volunteers		
Outreach area volunteers		

20. List the pastors and their length of tenure for the past twenty-five years. **Official Body Worksheet** (GT)

Organization:

21. Provide an official diagram of the decision-making and accountability structure of your congregation. **Official Body Worksheet** (LP)

22. Remember or imagine any creative new mission idea the church has implemented at one time or might implement in the future. Without reference to any official diagram of church structure, describe or draw how that idea would be approved and implemented. (**Note:** Gather as many responses from the Worship Survey Worksheet as possible and append them to this report.) **Worship Worksheet** (PF, LP)

23. Attach the job descriptions or sample mandates for the following individuals and groups: pastor, program staff, personnel committee, worship committee, cell group, and mission team. **Official Body Worksheet** (PF, LP, GT, SF)

24. What is the total number of hours volunteers spend each month in any administrative meetings? (This excludes time spent in training or actually doing ministries.) **Staff Worksheet** (SF, GT)

January	___	July	___
February	___	August	___
March	___	September	___
April	___	October	___
May	___	November	___
June	___	December	___

25. What is the total number of hours the church's program staff spends each month in any administrative meetings? (This excludes time spent in training or actually doing ministries.) **Staff Worksheet** (SF, GT)

January	___	July	___
February	___	August	___
March	___	September	___
April	___	October	___
May	___	November	___
June	___	December	___

26. Describe a controversy in the past five years and the internal congregational grievance process used to resolve it. **Official Body Worksheet** (AJ)

27. What is the long-range plan of the congregation? **Staff Worksheet** (CC, EH)

28. What are the *key issues, obstacles,* or *opportunities* facing the congregation in the next ten years? **Staff Worksheet, Official Body Worksheet** (CC, EH)

	Staff Perspective	**Official Body Perspective**
Key issues		
Key obstacles		
Key opportunities		

29. What is the makeup of the core leadership? (**Note:** The core leadership includes elected officers and volunteer leaders of groups, teams, classes, or other established organizational units.) **Official Body Worksheet** (GT)

Average age of elected officers:	___
Average age of core leaders in general:	___
Average length of congregational membership:	___
Average length of office tenure:	___
Percentage of core leaders age 14-18:	___
Percentage of core leaders age 19-35:	___
Percentage of core leaders age 35-50:	___
Percentage of core leaders age 51-65:	___
Percentage of core leaders age 65 and over:	___
Percentage male:	___
Percentage female:	___

30. From the perspective of others, is the pastor considered a leader? (**Note:** Record the average score from each worksheet on a 1-10 scale with 1 being a definite "no" and 10 being a wholehearted "yes.") **Staff, Official Body, and Worship Worksheets** (PF, SF)

	Causes things to happen.	***Really gets people moving.***	***Sees deep and far.***	***Takes risks and experiments with new ideas.***	***Builds bridges between opposite views and diverse ideas.***
Staff perspective					
Official body perspective					
Worshipers perspective					

Function

Changing People

31. What kind of worship options does your congregation offer? (**Note:** Complete a chart for each worship service offered. Whenever possible include a sample order of worship or a video clip of the service.) **Staff Worksheet** (PF, GT)

	Worship Service #1	*Worship Service #2*	*Worship Service #3*
Day and time?			
Location?			
Floor plan and furniture?			
Crucial technology?			
Kind of music?			
Musical instruments?			
Degree of formality?			
What group do you target?			
What need, yearning, or issue do you address?			
What leadership is necessary?			
How many weeks of the year is it offered?			
What is the average attendance in November?			
How many weeks is simultaneous child care provided?			
What kind of refreshments are offered?			

32. Chart the *average monthly attendance* of each worship service. **Staff Worksheet, Worship Worksheet** (PF, SF)

Service	Jan	Feb	Mar	Apr	May	June	July	Aug	Sept	Oct	Nov	Dec
1												
2												
3												

33. What benefit do people receive from each worship service? (**Note:** Record the average score from each worksheet on a 1-10 scale with 1 being extremely negative and 10 being extremely positive. Duplicate for additional services if necessary.) **Staff, Official Body, and Worship Worksheets, Random Survey** (CC, EH, SF)

Service #1	Personal transformation factor	Personal support factor	Motivation for spiritual growth factor	Education and learning factor	Mission connection factor
Staff perspective					
Official body perspective					
Worship perspective					
Random survey					

Service #2	Personal transformation factor	Personal support factor	Motivation for spiritual growth factor	Education and learning factor	Mission connection factor
Staff perspective					
Official body perspective					
Worship perspective					
Random survey					

Service #3	Personal transformation factor	Personal support factor	Motivation for spiritual growth factor	Education and learning factor	Mission connection factor
Staff perspective					
Official body perspective					
Worship perspective					
Random survey					

34. What worship design and leadership teams do you nurture? **Staff Worksheet** (SF, GT)

Team	Selection Method	Training Provided
Choirs		
Bands		
Readers		
Sacramental celebrants		
Dancers		
Preachers or Speakers		
Other		

35. What worship support teams do you nurture? **Staff Worksheet** (SF, GT)

Team	Selection Method	Training Provided
Valet parking		
Bus drivers		
Greeters		
Ushers		
Counselors		
Prayer partners		
Technology crews		
Interior decorators		
Other		

36. How many baptisms have been celebrated for each of the last ten years? **Staff Worksheet** (EH)

	Adult Baptisms	Teen Baptisms (related to membership)	Infant Baptisms
Current Year			
Last Year			
Two years ago			
Three years ago			
Four years ago			
Five years ago			
Six years ago			
Seven years ago			
Eight years ago			
Nine years ago			

37. What is the average breakdown of worshipers from Sundays during last November and last April? **Worship Worksheet** (PF)

Service	% of worshipers who are members	% of worshipers who attend regularly	% of worshipers who are *not* members or newcomers
1			
2			
3			

38. What are the five most memorable experiences (positive or negative) from worship services in the past year? **Worship Worksheet** (PF, CC, EH, AJ)

What happened?	Why was it so memorable?

39. How does the congregation respond to newcomers in worship? **Staff Worksheet** (LP, AJ)

- How do you know who is new?
- Who welcomes the newcomer?
- Who follows up with a visit?
- How soon is the visit usually done?

40. How do people rate your worship leadership? (**Note:** Combine scores from *all* worksheets and record the *average score* on a 1-10 scale with 1 being extremely negative and 10 being extremely positive.) **Staff, Official Body, and Worship Worksheets, Random Survey** (LP, GT, SF)

Leader(s)	**Sincerity**	**Spiritual depth**	**Skills**	**Approachability and friendliness**	**Team cooperation**
Preacher					
Organist					
Liturgists					
Band musicians					
Choir members					
Greeters					
Ushers					
Others					

Growing Christians

41. How far are participants willing to drive to church? **Worship Worksheet, Random Survey** (EH)

	% drive less than 1 mile	**% drive 1 – 3 miles**	**% drive 4 – 6 miles**	**% drive 7 –9 miles**	**% drive 10 – 15 miles**	**% drive more than 15 miles**
To work						
To shop						
To church						

42. Rate the importance of these expectations of membership in the church (1—high, 2—medium, 3—low) **Official Body Worksheet** (SF)

Regular worship attendance	___	Cell group participation	___
Percentage giving	___	Personal mission involvement	___
Tithing	___	Public confession of faith	___
Spiritual disciplines	___	Organizational leadership	___

Other expectations: ________________________________

43. What percent of newcomers in the past five years became active in the church? (**Note:** To be active in the church means to fulfill the minimum expectations of membership.) **Staff Worksheet** (LP)

44. Is the nursery meeting the expectations of the parents? (**Note:** Record the *average score* from each worksheet on a 1-10 scale with 1 being poor and 10 being perfect.) **Worship Worksheet, Random Survey** (CC, EH)

	Worship	**Random**		**Worship**	**Random**
Sufficient cribs	___	___	Security	___	___
Space for toddlers	___	___	Light, heat, and water	___	___
Separation of infants and toddlers	___	___	Staffing	___	___
Accessibility	___	___	Equipment	___	___

45. What opportunities do you provide for the personal, relational, and spiritual growth of adults? **Staff Worksheet** (AJ, SF)

Opportunity	**Who provides leadership?**	**How many were involved in the last twelve months?**
Spiritual gifts discernment		
Personality inventories		
Lifestyle coaching		
Mental health		
Emotional health		
Life skills development		
Premarriage counseling		
Intimacy enrichment		
Parenting		
Fellowship		
Twelve step support		
Mission awareness		
Bible study		
Faith formation		
Other		

46. How many adult spiritual development options do you have in the congregation? **Official Body Worksheet** (SF)

Development Option	**# during the week**	**# on Sunday**	**Average attendance**
Cell groups			
Large groups			
Classes			
Personal disciplines			
Mentoring partnerships			
Other			

47. What leader and staff training do you offer on a regular basis? **Staff Worksheet** (SF)

Opportunity	Who provides the training?
Listening	
Visitation	
Conflict resolution	
Interpersonal relations	
Prayer	
Bible	
Small group leadership	
Prayer and worship	
Other	

48. Rate the quality of lay leadership for nurturing personal, relational, and spiritual growth. (**Note:** Record the *average score* from each worksheet on a 1-10 scale with 1 being extremely negative and 10 being extremely positive.) **Staff, Official Body, and Worship Worksheets, Random Survey** (SF, GT)

Staff perspective ___ *Worshipers perspective* ___
Official body perspective ___ *Random survey* ___

49. Rate the quality of pastoral leadership for nurturing personal, relational, and spiritual growth. (**Note:** Record the *average score* from each worksheet on a 1-10 scale with 1 being extremely negative and 10 being extremely positive.) **Staff, Official Body, and Worship Worksheets, Random Survey** (PF, GT)

Staff perspective ___ *Worshipers perspective* ___
Official body perspective ___ *Random survey* ___

50. Describe a time of crisis or confusion during your life. What person within the church helped you resolve or overcome it? **Worship Worksheet** (EH, AJ)

Time of crisis	The person in the church who helped me

Discerning Call:

51. What percent of the congregation is committed to a discipline of spiritual growth that includes more than table grace (for example, daily prayer, Bible reading, conversation about faith, theological reading, lifestyle adjustments, innovation, and experimentation)? **Staff Worksheet, Worship Worksheet, Random Survey** (SF)

Staff perspective ___
Worship perspective ___
Random survey ___

52. List several creative ideas that emerged spontaneously in congregational life over the past five years—*and did not emerge from a strategic plan or committee meeting.* **Official Body Worksheet** (PF, EH)

This is the creative idea.	This is what happened to that idea.

53. Do congregational leaders understand themselves to be *called into a ministry* or *recruited to do a task?* (**Note:** Record the *average score* from each worksheet on a 1-10 scale with 1 signifying "task only" and 10 signifying "call only.") **Staff, Official Body, and Worship Worksheets** (PF, SF)

Staff perspective ___
Official body perspective ___
Worshipers perspective ___

54. Are congregational leaders perceived to be *anxious* or *open* about creative new ideas? (**Note:** Record the *average score* from each worksheet on a 1-10 scale with 1 signifying "very anxious" and 10 signifying "very open.") **Staff, Official Body, and Worship Worksheets** (LP, GT)

Staff perspective ___
Official body perspective ___
Worshipers perspective ___

55. Are congregational leaders perceived to be *fearful* or *daring* about taking a stand on controversial issues? (**Note:** Record the *average score* from each worksheet on a 1-10 scale with 1 signifying "very fearful" and 10 signifying "very daring.") **Staff, Official Body, and Worship Worksheets** (AJ)

Staff perspective ___
Official body perspective ___
Worshipers perspective ___

56. What method does the congregation use to learn from mistakes or failures? **Official Body Worksheet** (SF)

57. Do congregation leaders have a regular prayer and visioning retreat? **Official Body Worksheet** (PF, EH)

How often	% of Congregational leaders who attend
Annual	
Biannual	
Triannual	
Occasional	

58. How do congregational leaders intentionally listen to marginal members and the spiritually yearning, institutionally alienated public? **Staff Worksheet, Official Body Worksheet** (EH)

59. Does participation in congregational life influence lifestyle and career? (**Note:** Record the *average score* from each worksheet on a 1-10 scale with 1 signifying "no influence at all" and 10 signifying "enormous influence.") **Worship Worksheet, Random Survey** (SF)

	Lifestyle	**Career**
Worshipers perspective:	____	____
Random survey	____	____

60. How do staff members help others discern *their own* calling or ministry? (**Note:** Include a response from both program *and* support staff. Focus on deliberate disciplines or repeatable methods.) **Staff Worksheet** (SF, GT)

How the *pastor* does it:

How the *program* staff do it:

How the *support* staff do it:

Equipping Disciples:

61. How much money is dedicated to training laity? **Official Body Worksheet** (LP)

Total budget	Amount for lay continuing education	% of total budget

62. How much money is dedicated to training staff? **Staff Worksheet** (SF)

Total budget	Amount for staff continuing education	% of total budget

63. List the training opportunities for small and large group leaders. **Staff Worksheet** (LP)

Training opportunity	How often during the year	Who leads it?

64. List the training opportunities for program leaders and mission teams. **Staff Worksheet** (CC, AJ)

Training opportunity	How often during the year	Who leads it?

65. List the training opportunities for church members to share faith with friends, relatives, work associates, and neighbors. **Staff Worksheet** (GT)

Training opportunity	How often during the year	Who leads it?

66. How do social service missions by the congregation communicate their faith motivation to the general public? **Staff Worksheet** (CC, AJ)

67. How does the congregation train volunteers to work sensitively with other cultures, ethnic groups, or minorities in their local community or global partnerships? **Staff Worksheet** (AJ, CC)

68. How does the congregation recognize, commission, and prayerfully support emerging mission volunteers? **Staff Worksheet** (SF, GT)

69. Who monitors volunteer performance and targets appropriate standards of quality? **Staff Worksheet** (LP)

70. How much time and energy does the pastor give to empowering lay ministries? (**Note:** Record the *average score* from each worksheet on a 1-10 scale as indicated below.) **Staff Worksheet, Worship Worksheet, Random Survey** (CC, LP)

	Is the pastor doing ministry alone (1) or mentoring apprentices to do that ministry (10)?	Is the pastor doing tasks on behalf of the church (1) or training others to do the same work (10)?	Is the pastor counseling with individuals (1) or coaching in groups (10)?
Staff perspective			
Worshipers perspective			
Random survey			

Deploying Servants:

71. List all of the missions and ministries related to your congregation and see how church members related to them. **Staff Worksheet** (GT, CC, AJ)

Mission or Ministry	Property use only (free use or rental)	Financial support only	Church members set policy	Church members participate in the mission	Approximate # of church members involved	# of staff or church leaders involved

72. How many church members involved in the missions and ministries of the church regularly attend worship? **Worship Worksheet** (SF)

73. How many visitors to worship came as a result of a particular mission or ministry of the church? (Estimate percentage of total worshipers each year) **Worship Worksheet** (CC, EH)

74. Does worship regularly focus prayer or celebration on one or more of the missions or ministries listed in question 71? **Staff Worksheet** (CC)

75. What percent of the church members are involved in some way with a ministry or mission of the church? **Official Body Worksheet** (CC, AJ)

Fund raising only	Administration	Hands-on involvement

76. Are volunteers generally deployed as *true teams* or *task groups*? (**Note:** Circle the number in each continuum that best describes how volunteer groups are deployed.) **Official Body Worksheet** (LP)

<u>**True Teams**</u>	*Circle the number in each category*	<u>**Task Groups**</u>
Discerns emerging mission by itself	**1 2 3 4 5 6 7 8 9 10**	Addresses the mission perceived by the board or clergy
Designs strategies to address mission on its own	**1 2 3 4 5 6 7 8 9 10**	Follows direction describing how to address the mission
Implements mission strategies without asking permission	**1 2 3 4 5 6 7 8 9 10**	Submits recommended strategies for approval
Evaluates mission results on its own	**1 2 3 4 5 6 7 8 9 10**	Presents reports to board or clergy for evaluation
Performs both social action and faith witness	**1 2 3 4 5 6 7 8 9 10**	Executes tasks without articulating faith motivation
Leader emerges from spiritual growth processes of the congregation	**1 2 3 4 5 6 7 8 9 10**	Leader nominated or appointed by administrative meeting

77. How does the church know if volunteers have gone beyond the boundaries of congregational identity (core values, beliefs, vision, and mission)? **Official Body Worksheet** (PF, LP)

78. How does the church know what the general public thinks of the church? **Official Body Worksheet** (AJ, CC, EH)

79. Does the church create a welcome and inclusive environment for the diverse lifestyles of the public? (**Note:** Record the *average score* from each worksheet on a 1-10 scale with 1 being extremely negative and 10 being extremely positive.) **Official Body Worksheet, Worship Worksheet, Random Survey** (AJ)

Official body perspective ___
Worshipers perspective ___
Random survey ___

80. Do church officers and mission leaders regularly speak of their spiritual journey and faith motivation in worship or other community settings? **Official Body Worksheet** (EH, SF)

Form

Property:

81. Do the trustees and property managers understand their job as *the maintenance of church assets* or *the resourcing of congregational mission*? (**Note:** Record the *average score* from each worksheet on a 1-10 scale with 1 signifying "maintenance" and 10 signifying "resourcing.") **Official Body Worksheet, Worship Worksheet, Random Survey** (LP, GT)

Official body perspective	___
Worshipers perspective	___
Random survey	___

82. Provide an exterior site plan and interior floor plan of the church. **Official Body Worksheet** (LP)

Size of land	
Number of on-site parking spaces	
Sanctuary seating capacity	
Indoor or outdoor athletic facilities	
Housing for staff	
Other properties	
Handicapped accessibility	

83. Are church signs adequate on and around church property? **Official Body Worksheet** (CC, LP)

Visible to cars traveling the speed limit?	
Illuminated?	
Easy to change?	
Located at major intersections to the maximum radius people travel to church?	

84. What are the major interior and exterior symbols designed to capture the attention of visitors and worshipers? **Official Body Worksheet** (PF)

85. Is the sanctuary adequate for multiple worship options? **Official Body Worksheet** (CC, LP)

Worship occasionally over 80 percent seating capacity?	
Pews or flexible seating?	
Upgraded electrical service?	
Available musical instruments?	
Moveable chancel or stage furniture?	
Adjustable lighting?	
Air quality?	
Describe the audio system	
Describe the video system	

86. Is the refreshment and fellowship center adequate? **Official Body Worksheet** (CC, LP)

This area is what percent of the size of the sanctuary?	
How many serving stations?	
How large are display areas?	
Is there an adjacent resource center?	
Is this area linked physically or electronically to the nursery?	
Is there an automated bank teller?	
Describe the food typically served.	

87. Is the office space adequate? **Official Body Worksheet** (LP)

Conveniently located?	
Secure view of entrances?	
Protect confidentiality?	
Hospitable to visitors?	
Computer linked?	

88. Is the education space adequate? **Official Body Worksheet** (SF)

How many nonclassroom, "parlor" style rooms?	
Attendance occasionally over 80 percent seating capacity?	
Technology equivalent to public school?	
Safe, healthy environments?	

89. What are the most recent property and technology upgrades in the last ten years? **Official Body Worksheet** (CC, SF)

90. Describe exactly what a visitor sees upon walking into the main entrance of the building. **Official Body Worksheet** (PF)

Finance:

91. Do the treasurers and financial managers understand their job as *the maintenance of church assets* or *the resourcing of congregational mission*? (**Note:** Record the *average score* from each worksheet on a 1-10 scale with 1 signifying "maintenance" and 10 signifying "resourcing.") **Official Body Worksheet, Worship Worksheet, Random Survey** (CC, LP)

Official body perspective ___
Worshipers perspective ___
Random survey ___

92. Provide financial information for the past ten years. **Official Body Worksheet** (All)

Year	Total operating budget	Salaries	Program expenses	Denomination mission contributions	All other mission contributions	Debt retirement	Annual deficit or surplus
Current year							
Last year							

93. How does the congregation address annual deficits or surpluses? **Official Body Worksheet** (GT, EH)

94. List all financial reserves, endowments, or annual grants received. **Official Body Worksheet** (GT, EH)

95. Summarize the congregational stewardship strategy. **Official Body Worksheet** (CC, AJ)

Annual campaign?	
Percentage giving?	
Tithing?	
List optional giving methods	
List optional giving targets	

96. Summarize any financial capital campaign the congregation has done in the past five years. **Official Body Worksheet** (EH, GT)

Purpose	
Date	
Method	
Result	

97. Compare the *average weekly* giving of members and leaders. **Staff, Official Body, and Worship Worksheets** (GT, CC)

Staff giving: __________
Elected officer giving: __________
Worshiper giving: __________

98. Is staff compensation comparable to equivalent positions in the community? **Official Body Worksheet** (LP, AJ)

99. Is the pastor's compensation above or below the minimum denominational guidelines? Is it above or below the median compensation of other pastors in the community? **Official Body Worksheet** (LP, AJ)

100. Does the congregation ask for money to *keep the doors open* or *open new doors*? (**Note:** Record the *average score* from each worksheet on a 1-10 scale.) **Official Body Worksheet, Worship Worksheet, Random Survey** (CC)

Official body perspective: ___
Worshipers perspective: ___
Random survey: ___

Communication:

101. To whom are the ministries and missions of the congregation aimed? **Official Body Worksheet** (CC, AJ)

Ministry or Mission	The people it is directed toward	The results we hope to generate

102. What are the membership trends for the past ten years? **Staff Worksheet, Worship Worksheet, Random Survey** (PF, EH)

	Total members beginning year	Removed by death	Removed by transfer or other means	Received by affirmation of faith	Received by transfer or other means	Total members year end
Current year						
Last year						
Two years ago						
Three years ago						
Four years ago						
Five years ago						
Six years ago						
Seven years ago						
Eight years ago						
Nine years ago						

% of questionnaires returned compared to total congregational participation	
% of total questionnaires returned that were from *members*	
% of total questionnaires returned that were from *nonmembers*	

103. What media is used to communicate within and beyond the church? **Staff Worksheet** (LP)

	Within the church	Beyond the church
Direct mail		
Door-to-door visitation		
Newsletters		
Videotapes		
Sunday announcements		
Bulletin inserts or handouts		
Computer networks		
Posters		
Cable television		
Newspapers		
Radio		
Billboard, bus, park bench advertising		
Other		

104. How do we use the holidays listed below to communicate to the public and draw them toward the church? **Official Body Worksheet** (PF, EH)

Christmas Eve:

Valentines Day:

Easter:

Mother's Day:

Thanksgiving:

Halloween:

105. How are editors, producers, or other leaders of communication networks selected and trained? **Staff Worksheet** (LP)

106. List the mission partners with whom the congregation interacts regularly. **Staff Worksheet** (CC, AJ)

	Mission Partners	**Is there an interactive display visible in the foyer or fellowship center?**
Global		
Ecumenical		
Denominational		
Interfaith		
Corporate		
Government		
Social Service		

107. Are designated staff or laity equipped to relate to segments of the public in the appropriate languages and cultural forms? **Staff Worksheet** (CC, AJ)

108. Is the church secretary chosen, trained, and deployed for quality interaction with the public? (**Note:** Record the *average score* from each worksheet on a 1-10 scale with 1 being extremely negative and 10 being extremely positive.) **Official Body Worksheet, Worship Worksheet, Random Survey** (LP, GT)

Official body perspective ___
Worshipers perspective ___
Random survey ___

109. In ten words or less, what is the core message you always project beyond the church? **Official Body Worksheet** (PF, EH)

110. What comments do participants make that might help leaders prepare for the future? **Worship Worksheet, Random Survey** (ALL)

OFFICIAL BODY WORKSHEET

After completing the worksheet, transfer the data to the master congregational mission assessment form. Occasionally, staff answers will be correlated with responses from other worksheets. The number in bold parenthesis **(#)** indicates the question number on the master assessment form.

Foundation

Genetic Code:

1. **(5)** What are the core values of the congregation? A *core value* is the positive preference or choice congregational participants make, both habitually and daringly, in daily living.

   Official body perspective:

   1.
   2.
   3.
   4.
   5.

2. **(6)** What are the bedrock beliefs of the congregation? A *bedrock belief* is the principle, symbol, or faith story that congregational participants return to for strength in times of confusion or stress.

   Official body perspective:

   1.
   2.
   3.
   4.
   5.

3. **(7)** What is the motivating vision of the congregation? A *motivating vision* is the song, image, picture, or symbol, the mere recollection of which elicits joy, shapes personal lifestyle, and demands to be shared with strangers.

   Official body perspective:

4. **(8)** What is the key mission of the congregation? A *key mission* is everything that needs to be said about the church to invite enormous congregational courage and excite the imagination of the public—and can be printed on the side of a city bus.

   Official body perspective:

Core Leadership:

5. **(11)** Identify all salaried staff (part- and full-time, honorarium or full benefits).

Position	Part- or Full-time	Honorarium or Benefits	Current Salary

6. **(12)** In the perspective of others, does the pastor model the values, beliefs, vision, and mission of the congregation? **(Note:** Record the average score on a 1-10 scale with 1 being an outright "no" and 10 being a wholehearted "yes.")

   Official body perspective: ____

7. **(13)** Does the official body of elected officers model the values, beliefs, vision, and mission of the congregation? (**Note:** Record the average score on a 1-10 scale with 1 being an outright "no" and 10 being a wholehearted "yes.")

   Official body perspective: ____

8. **(14)** In the perspective of others, do the core leaders of group, program, or ministry volunteers model the values, beliefs, vision, and mission of the congregation? (**Note:** Record the average score on a 1-10 scale with 1 being an outright "no" and 10 being a wholehearted "yes.")

   Official body perspective: ____

9. **(15)** *How* does the pastor invest his or her time and energy? (**Note:** Record the *average percentages* from each column. Do a separate report for each associate or team "pastor." The total perspective should equal 100 percent.)

	Position Title:	**% of energy on church members**	**% of energy on non-members**	**% of energy on personal growth**	**% of energy on denominational duties**	**% of energy on other personal and family issues**
Official body perspective						

10. **(16)** *How* do core leaders who work in each of the following program areas invest their time and energy? (**Note:** Record the *average percentages* from each column of each worksheet. Do a separate report for each staff position, such as organist, choir director, drama coordinator, Christian education director, youth minister, pastoral visitor, and so on.)

WORSHIP PROGRAM	**Position Title:**	**% of energy on church members**	**% of energy on non-members**	**% of energy on personal growth**	**% of energy on denominational duties**	**% of energy on other personal and family issues**
Official body perspective						

EDUCATION PROGRAM	Position Title:	% of energy on church members	% of energy on non-members	% of energy on personal growth	% of energy on denominational duties	% of energy on other personal and family issues
Official body perspective						

VISITATION PROGRAM	Position Title:	% of energy on church members	% of energy on non-members	% of energy on personal growth	% of energy on denominational duties	% of energy on other personal and family issues
Official body perspective						

11. **(17)** Rank, in order of importance, how the congregation discovers and appoints volunteers?

Nominations processes ___
Formal interviews ___
Appointments ___
Appeals to fill vacancies ___
Time/Talent inventories ___
Gifts discernment inventories ___
Personality inventories ___
Call discernment processes ___
Other ______________________________

12. **(18)** How does the congregation train and equip church leaders?

Position or Program	Is initial training required?	Average initial training time	Is follow-up training required?	Average follow-up training time	Who does the training?	Budget for training
Pastor						Training budget for staff:
Program staff						
Support staff						
Worship area volunteers						Training budget for volunteers:
Education area volunteers						
Visitation area volunteers						
Outreach area volunteers						

13. **(19)** What methods and resources are used in training church leaders?

Position or Program	What resources are used?	What teaching methods are used?
Pastor		
Program staff		
Support staff		
Worship area volunteers		
Education area volunteers		
Visitation area volunteers		
Outreach area volunteers		

14. **(20)** List the pastors and length of tenure for the past twenty-five years.

Organization:

15. **(21)** Provide an official diagram of the decision making and accountability structure of your congregation.

16. **(23)** Attach the job descriptions or sample mandates for the following individuals and groups: pastor, program staff, personnel committee, worship committee, cell group, and mission team.

17. **(26)** Describe a controversy in the past five years and the internal congregational grievance process used to resolve it.

18. **(28)** What are the *key issues, obstacles,* or *opportunities* facing the congregation in the next ten years?

Official body perspective	
Key issues	
Key obstacles	
Key opportunities	

19. **(29)** What is the makeup of the core leadership? (**Note:** The core leadership includes elected officers and volunteer leaders of groups, teams, classes, or other established organizational units.)

Average age of elected officers: ___
Average age of core leaders in general: ___
Average length of congregational membership: ___
Average length of office tenure: ___
Percentage age 14-18: ___
Percentage age 19-35: ___
Percentage age 35-50: ___
Percentage age 51-65: ___
Percentage age 65 and over: ___
Percentage male: ___
Percentage female: ___

20. **(30)** From the perspective of others, is the pastor considered a leader? (**Note:** Record the *average score* on a 1-10 scale with 1 being a definite "no" and 10 being a wholehearted "yes.")

	Causes things to happen.	**Really gets people moving.**	**Sees deep and far.**	**Takes risks and experiments with new ideas.**	**Builds bridges between opposite views and diverse ideas.**
Official body perspective					

Function

Changing People:

21. **(33)** What benefit do people receive from each worship service? (**Note:** Record the *average score* on a 1-10 scale with 1 being extremely negative and 10 being extremely positive. Duplicate for additional services if necessary.)

Service #1	**Personal transformation factor**	**Personal support factor**	**Motivation for spiritual growth factor**	**Education and learning factor**	**Mission connection factor**
Official body perspective					

Service #2	Personal transformation factor	Personal support factor	Motivation for spiritual growth factor	Education and learning factor	Mission connection factor
Official body perspective					

Service #3	Personal transformation factor	Personal support factor	Motivation for spiritual growth factor	Education and learning factor	Mission connection factor
Official body perspective					

22. **(40)** How do people rate your worship leadership? (**Note:** Record the *average score* on a 1-10 scale with 1 being extremely negative and 10 being extremely positive.)

Leader(s)	Sincerity	Spiritual depth	Skills	Approachability and friendliness	Team cooperation
Preacher					
Organist					
Liturgists					
Band musicians					
Choir members					
Greeters					
Ushers					
Others					

Growing Christians:

23. **(42)** Rate the importance of these expectations of membership in the church (1—high, 2—medium, 3—low)

Regular worship attendance	___	Cell group participation	___
Percentage giving	___	Personal mission involvement	___
Tithing	___	Public confession of faith	___
Spiritual disciplines	___	Organizational leadership	___

Other expectations: ____

24. **(46)** How many adult spiritual development options do you have in the congregation?

Development Option	# during the week	# on Sunday	Average attendance
Cell groups			
Large groups			
Classes			
Personal disciplines			
Mentoring partnerships			
Other			

25. **(48)** Rate the quality of *lay* leadership for nurturing personal, relational, and spiritual growth. (**Note:** Record the average score on a 1-10 scale with 1 being extremely negative and 10 being extremely positive.)

Official body perspective ___

26. **(49)** Rate the quality of *pastoral* leadership for nurturing personal, relational, and spiritual growth. (**Note:** Record the average score on a 1-10 scale with 1 being extremely negative and 10 being extremely positive.)

Official body perspective ___

Discerning Call:

27. **(52)** List several creative ideas that emerged spontaneously in congregational life over the past five years—and *did not emerge from a strategic plan or committee meeting.*

This is the creative idea.	This is what happened to that idea.

28. **(53)** Do congregational leaders understand themselves to be *called into a ministry* or *recruited to do a task*? (**Note:** Record the *average score* on a 1-10 scale with 1 signifying "task only" and 10 signifying "call only.")

Official body perspective ___

29. **(54)** Are congregational leaders perceived to be *anxious* or *open* about creative new ideas? (**Note:** Record the *average score* on a 1-10 scale with 1 signifying "very anxious" and 10 signifying "very open.")

Official body perspective ___

30. **(55)** Are congregational leaders perceived to be *fearful* or *daring* about taking a stand on controversial issues? (**Note:** Record the *average score* on a 1-10 scale with 1 signifying "very fearful" and 10 signifying "very daring.")

Official body perspective ___

31. **(56)** What method does the congregation use to learn from mistakes or failures?

32. **(57)** Do congregational leaders have a regular prayer and visioning retreat?

How often	% of congregational leaders who attend
Annual	
Biannual	
Triannual	
Occasional	

33. **(58)** How do congregational leaders intentionally listen to marginal members and the spiritually yearning, institutionally alienated public?

Equipping Disciples:

34. **(61)** How much money is dedicated to training laity?

Total Budget	Amount for lay continuing education	% of total budget

Deploying Servants:

35. **(75)** What percent of the church members are involved in some way with a ministry or mission of the church?

Fund raising only	Administration	Hands-on involvement

36. **(76)** Are volunteers generally deployed as *true teams* or *task groups*? (**Note:** Circle the number in each continuum that best describes how volunteer groups are deployed.)

True Teams	*Circle the number in each category*	**Task Groups**
Discerns emerging mission by itself	**1 2 3 4 5 6 7 8 9 10**	Addresses the mission perceived by the board or clergy
Designs strategies to address mission on its own	**1 2 3 4 5 6 7 8 9 10**	Follows directions describing how to address the mission
Implements mission strategies without asking permission	**1 2 3 4 5 6 7 8 9 10**	Submits recommended strategies for approval
Evaluates mission results on its own	**1 2 3 4 5 6 7 8 9 10**	Presents reports to board or clergy for evaluation

Performs both social action and faith witness	**1 2 3 4 5 6 7 8 9 10**	Executes tasks without articulating faith motivation
Leader emerges from spiritual growth processes of the congregation	**1 2 3 4 5 6 7 8 9 10**	Leader nominated or appointed by administrative meeting

37. **(77)** How does the church know if volunteers have gone beyond the boundaries of congregational identity (core values, beliefs, vision, and mission)?

38. **(78)** How does the church know what the general public thinks of the church?

39. **(79)** Does the church create a welcome and inclusive environment for the diverse lifestyles of the public? (**Note:** Record the average score on a 1-10 scale with 1 being extremely negative and 10 being extremely positive.)

    Official body perspective: ___

40. **(80)** Do church officers and mission leaders regularly speak of their spiritual journey and faith motivation in worship or other community settings?

Form

Property:

41. **(81)** Do the trustees and property managers understand their job as *the maintenance of church assets* or *the resourcing of congregational mission*? (**Note:** Record the *average score* on a 1-10 scale with 1 signifying "maintenance" and 10 signifying "resourcing.")

    Official body perspective ___

42. **(82)** Provide an exterior site plan and interior floor plan of the church.

Size of land	
Number of on-site parking spaces	
Sanctuary seating capacity	
Indoor or outdoor athletic facilities	
Housing for staff	
Other properties	
Handicapped accessibility	

43. **(83)** Are church signs adequate on and around church property?

Visible to cars traveling the speed limit?	
Illuminated?	
Easy to change?	
Located at major intersections to the maximum radius people travel to church?	

44. **(84)** What are the major interior and exterior symbols designed to capture the attention of visitors and worshipers?

45. **(85)** Is the sanctuary adequate for multiple worship options?

Worship occasionally over 80 percent seating capacity?	
Pews or flexible seating?	
Upgraded electrical service?	
Available musical instruments?	
Movable chancel or stage furniture?	
Adjustable lighting?	
Air quality?	
Describe the audio system	
Describe the video system	

46. **(86)** Is the refreshment and fellowship center adequate?

This area is what % of the size of the sanctuary?	
How many serving stations?	
How large are display areas?	
Is there an adjacent resource center?	
Is this area linked physically or electronically to the nursery?	
Is there an automated bank teller?	
Describe the food typically served.	

47. **(87)** Is the office space adequate?

Conveniently located?	
Secure view of entrances?	
Protect confidentiality?	
Hospitable to visitors?	
Computer linked?	

48. **(88)** Is the education space adequate?

How many nonclassroom, "parlor" style rooms?	
Attendance occasionally over 80 percent seating capacity?	
Technology equivalent to public school?	
Safe, healthy environments?	

49. **(89)** What are the most recent property and technology upgrades in the last ten years?

50. **(90)** Describe exactly what a visitor sees upon walking into the main entrance of the building?

Finance:

51. **(91)** Do the treasurers and financial managers understand their job as *the maintenance of church assets* or *the resourcing of congregational mission*? (**Note:** Record the *average score* on a 1-10 scale with 1 signifying "maintenance" and 10 signifying "resourcing.")

    Official body perspective: ___

52. **(92)** Provide financial information for the past ten years.

Year	**Total operating budget**	**Salaries**	**Program expenses**	**Denomination mission contributions**	**All other mission contributions**	**Debt retirement**	**Annual deficit or surplus**
Current year							
Last year							

53. **(93)** How does the congregation address annual deficits or surpluses?

54. **(94)** List all financial reserves, endowments, or annual grants received.

55. **(95)** Summarize the congregational stewardship strategy.

Annual campaign?	
Percentage giving?	
Tithing?	
List optional giving methods	
List optional giving targets	

56. **(96)** Summarize any financial capital campaign the congregation has done in the past five years.

Purpose	
Date	
Method	
Result	

57. **(97)** Compare the *average weekly* giving of members and leaders.

Average elected officer giving: _______

58. **(98)** Is staff compensation comparable to equivalent positions in the community?

59. **(99)** Is the pastor's compensation above or below the minimum denominational guidelines? Is it above or below the median compensation of other pastors in the community?

60. **(100)** Does the congregation ask for money to *keep the doors open* or *open new doors?* (**Note:** Record the *average score* on a 1-10 scale.)

Official body perspective: ___

Communication:

61. **(101)** To whom are the ministries and missions of the congregation aimed?

Ministry or Mission	The people it is directed toward	The results we hope to generate

62. **(104)** How do we use the holidays listed below to communicate to the public and draw them toward the church?

Christmas Eve:

Valentines Day:

Easter:

Mother's Day:

Thanksgiving:

Halloween:

63. **(108)** Is the church secretary chosen, trained, and deployed for quality interaction with the public? (**Note:** Record the *average score* on a 1-10 scale with 1 being extremely negative and 10 being extremely positive.)

Official body perspective ___

64. **(109)** In ten words or less, what is the core message you always project beyond the church?

STAFF WORKSHEET

After completing the worksheet, transfer the data to the master congregational mission assessment form. Occasionally, staff answers will be correlated with responses from other worksheets. The number in bold parenthesis **(#)** indicates the question number on the master assessment form.

Foundation

Genetic Code:

1. **(1)** What are the age, marital status, race or cultural origin, and educational level of adult worshipers? **(PF, CC, EH, AJ)**

Birth Years

Line		1966–1985 % of congregation	1946–1965 % of congregation	1936–1945 % of congregation	1915–1935 % of congregation	1900–1914 % of congregation
1	Total % in this age group					

Demographic Diversity

Line		% of adult worshipers		Line		% of adult worshipers
					Household Income:	
				7	Under $10,000	
1	**Married**				$10,000–29,999	
2	**Divorced/Separated**				$30,000–49,999	
3	**Widowed**				$50,000–69,999	
4	**Never married**				$70,000–89,999	
					Over $90,000	
5	**Households with children at home**					
				8	**Homeowners**	
				9	**Renters**	
6	**Cultural Background:**				**Education:**	
	Western European				Below high school	
	Eastern European				High school	
	African				College/University	
	Hispanic				Career training	
	Caribbean				Advanced degree	
	Asian					
	Pacific Rim			10	**Technology Use:**	
	Middle Eastern				Cell phone	
	Far Eastern				Computer	
	Native North American				Internet	
					Microwave	

2. **(1)** How does this compare with demographic statistics for our area? **(PF, CC, EH, AJ)**

Birth Years

Line		**1966–1985 % of population**	**1946–1965 % of population**	**1936–1945 % of population**	**1915–1935 % of population**	**1900–1914 % of population**
1	**Total % in this age group**					

Demographic Diversity

Line		**% of adult population**		**Line**		**% of adult population**
				7	**Household Income:** Under $10,000	
1	**Married**				$10,000–29,999	
2	**Divorced/Separated**				$30,000–49,999	
3	**Widowed**				$50,000–69,999	
4	**Never married**				$70,000–89,999	
					Over $90,000	
5	**Households with children at home**					
				8	**Homeowners**	
				9	**Renters**	
6	**Cultural Background:** Western European				**Education:** Below high school	
	Eastern European				High school	
	African				College/University	
	Hispanic				Career training	
	Caribbean				Advanced degree	
	Asian					
	Pacific Rim			**10**	**Technology Use:** Cell phone	
	Middle Eastern				Computer	
	Far Eastern				Internet	
	Native North American				Microwave	

3. **(5)** What are the core values of the congregation? A *core value* is the positive preference or choice congregational participants make, both habitually and daringly, in daily living.

Staff perspective:

1.
2.
3.
4.
5.

4. **(6)** What are the bedrock beliefs of the congregation? A *bedrock belief* is the principle, symbol, or faith story that congregational participants return to for strength in times of confusion or stress.

Staff perspective:

1.
2.
3.
4.
5.

5. **(7)** What is the motivating vision of the congregation? A *motivating vision* is the song, image, picture, or symbol, the mere recollection of which elicits joy, shapes personal lifestyle, and demands to be shared with strangers.

   Staff perspective:

6. **(8)** What is the key mission of the congregation? A *key mission* is everything that needs to be said about the church to invite enormous congregational courage and excite the imagination of the public—and can be printed on the side of a city bus.

   Staff perspective:

7. **(9)** How is the genetic code of identity (values, beliefs, vision, mission) embedded in every new member, leader, program, alternate worship service, and ministry of the congregation?

	Tactics	**Resources**
Each new member:		
Each leader:		
Each program:		
Each worship service:		
Each ministry:		

8. **(10)** How is the genetic code of identity (values, beliefs, vision, mission) communicated beyond the church?

	Tactics	**Resources**
To the general public:		
To the social service sector:		
To the government sector:		
To the business sector:		
To the education sector:		

Core Leadership:

9. **(12)** In the perspective of others, does the pastor model the values, beliefs, vision, and mission of the congregation? **(Note:** Record the *average score* on a 1-10 scale with 1 being an outright "no" and 10 being a wholehearted "yes.")

   Staff perspective: ___

10. **(13)** In the perspective of others, does the official body of elected officers model the values, beliefs, vision, and mission of the congregation? (**Note:** Record the *average score* on a 1-10 scale with 1 being an outright "no" and 10 being a wholehearted "yes.")

    Staff perspective: ___

11. **(14)** In the perspective of others, do the core leaders of group, program, or ministry volunteers model the values, beliefs, vision, and mission of the congregation? (**Note:** Record the *average score* on a 1-10 scale with 1 being an outright "no" and 10 being a wholehearted "yes.")

    Staff perspective: ___

12. **(15)** *How* does the pastor invest his or her time and energy? **(PF)** (**Note:** Record the *average percentages* from each column. Do a separate report for each associate or team "pastor." The total perspective should equal 100 percent.)

PASTOR(S)	**Position Title:**	**% of energy on church members**	**% of energy on non-members**	**% of energy on personal growth**	**% of energy on denominational duties**	**% of energy on other personal and family issues**
Official body perspective						

13. **(16)** *How* do core leaders who work in each of the following program areas invest their time and energy? **(GT)** (**Note:** Record the *average percentages* from each column of each worksheet. Do a separate report for each staff position, such as organist, choir director, drama coordinator, Christian education director, youth minister, counselor, pastoral visitor, and so on.)

WORSHIP PROGRAM	**Position Title:**	**% of energy on church members**	**% of energy on non-members**	**% of energy on personal growth**	**% of energy on denominational duties**	**% of energy on other personal and family issues**
Official body perspective						

EDUCATION PROGRAM	**Position Title:**	**% of energy on church members**	**% of energy on non-members**	**% of energy on personal growth**	**% of energy on denominational duties**	**% of energy on other personal and family issues**
Official body perspective						

VISITATION PROGRAM	Position Title:	% of energy on church members	% of energy on non-members	% of energy on personal growth	% of energy on denominational duties	% of energy on other personal and family issues
Official body perspective						

14. **(17)** Rank, in order of importance, how the congregation discovers and appoints volunteers. **(LP)**

Nominations processes ___
Formal interviews ___
Appointments ___
Appeals to fill vacancies ___
Time/Talent inventories ___
Gifts discernment inventories ___
Personality inventories ___
Call discernment processes ___
Other ______________________________

Organization:

15. **(24)** What is the total number of hours volunteers spend each month in any administrative meetings? (This *excludes* time spent in training or actually doing ministries.) **(SF, GT)**

January ___
February ___
March ___
April ___
May ___
June ___
July ___
August ___
September ___
October ___
November ___
December ___

16. **(25)** What is the total number of hours the church's program staff spends each month in any administrative meetings? (This *excludes* time spent in training or actually doing ministries.) **(SF, GT)**

January ___
February ___
March ___
April ___
May ___
June ___
July ___
August ___
September ___
October ___
November ___
December ___

17. **(27)** What is the long-range plan of the congregation?

18. **(28)** What are the *key issues, obstacles,* or *opportunities* facing the congregation in the next ten years? **(CC, EH)**

Staff Perspective	
Key issues	
Key obstacles	
Key opportunities	

19. **(30)** From the perspective of others, is the pastor considered a leader? (**Note:** Record the *average score* on a 1-10 scale with 1 being a definite "no" and 10 being a wholehearted "yes.") **(PF, SF)**

	Causes things to happen.	**Really gets people moving.**	**Sees deep and far.**	**Takes risks and experiments with new ideas.**	**Builds bridges between opposite views and diverse ideas.**
Staff perspective					

Function

Changing People:

20. **(31)** What kind of worship options does your congregation offer? (**Note:** Complete a chart for each worship service offered. Whenever possible include a sample order of worship or a video clip of the service). **(PF, GT)**

	Worship Service #1	*Worship Service #2*	*Worship Service #3*
Day and time?			
Location?			
Floor plan and furniture?			
Crucial technology?			
Kind of music?			
Musical instruments?			
Degree of formality?			
What group do you want to target?			
What need, yearning, or issue do you address?			
What leadership is necessary?			
How many weeks of the year is it offered?			
What is the average attendance in November?			
How many weeks is simultaneous child care provided?			
What kind of refreshments are offered?			

21. **(32)** Chart the *average monthly attendance* of each worship service.

Service	Jan	Feb	Mar	Apr	May	June	July	Aug	Sept	Oct	Nov	Dec
1												
2												
3												
4												
5												

22. **(33)** What benefit do people receive from each worship service? (**Note:** Record the *average score* from each worksheet on a 1-10 scale with 1 being extremely negative and 10 being extremely positive. Duplicate for additional services if necessary). **(CC, EH, SF)**

Service #1	Personal transformation factor	Personal support factor	Motivation for spiritual growth factor	Education and learning factor	Mission connection factor
Staff perspective					

Service #2	Personal transformation factor	Personal support factor	Motivation for spiritual growth factor	Education and learning factor	Mission connection factor
Staff perspective					

Service #3	Personal transformation factor	Personal support factor	Motivation for spiritual growth factor	Education and learning factor	Mission connection factor
Staff perspective					

23. **(34)** What worship design and leadership teams do you nurture?

Team	Selection Method	Training Provided
Choirs		
Bands		
Readers		
Sacramental celebrants		
Readers		
Dancers		
Preachers or Speakers		
Other		

24. **(35)** What worship support teams do you nurture?

Team	Selection Method	Training Provided
Valet parking		
Bus drivers		
Greeters		
Ushers		
Counselors		
Prayer partners		
Technology crews		
Interior decorators		
Other		

25. **(36)** How many baptisms have been celebrated for each of the last ten years? **(EH)**

	Adult Baptisms	**Teen Baptisms (related to membership)**	**Infant Baptisms**
Current Year			
Last Year			
Two years ago			
Three years ago			
Four years ago			
Five years ago			
Six years ago			
Seven years ago			
Eight years ago			
Nine years ago			

26. **(39)** How does the congregation respond to newcomers in worship? **(LP, AJ)**

- How do you know who is new?
- Who welcomes the newcomer?
- Who follows up with a visit?
- How soon is the visit usually done?

27. **(40)** How do people rate your worship leadership? (**Note:** Combine scores from *all* worksheets and record the *average score* on a 1-10 scale with 1 being extremely negative and 10 being extremely positive.) **(LP GT, SF)**

Leader(s)	**Sincerity**	**Spiritual depth**	**Skills**	**Approachability and friendliness**	**Team cooperation**
Preacher					
Organist					
Liturgists					
Band musicians					
Choir members					
Greeters					
Ushers					
Others					

Growing Christians:

28. **(43)** What percent of newcomers in the past five years became active in the church? (**Note:** To be active in the church means to fulfill the minimum expectations of membership.) **(LP)**

29. **(45)** What opportunities do you provide for the personal, relational, and spiritual growth of adults? **(AJ, SF)**

Opportunity	Who provides leadership?	How many involved in the last twelve months?
Spiritual gifts discernment		
Personality inventories		
Lifestyle coaching		
Mental health		
Emotional health		
Life skills development		
Premarriage counseling		
Intimacy enrichment		
Parenting		
Fellowship		
Twelve step support		
Mission awareness		
Bible study		
Faith formation		
Other		

30. **(47)** What leader and staff training do you offer on a regular basis? **(SF)**

Opportunity	Who is the leadership?
Listening	
Visitation	
Conflict resolution	
Interpersonal relations	
Prayer	
Bible	
Small group leadership	
Prayer and worship	
Other	

31. **(48)** Rate the quality of *lay* leadership for nurturing personal, relational, and spiritual growth. (**Note:** Record the *average score* on a 1-10 scale with 1 being extremely negative and 10 being extremely positive.)

    Staff perspective ___

32. **(49)** Rate the quality of *pastoral* leadership for nurturing personal, relational, and spiritual growth. (**Note:** Record the *average score* from each worksheet on a 1-10 scale with 1 being extremely negative and 10 being extremely positive.)

    Staff perspective ___

Discerning Call:

33. **(51)** What percent of the congregation is committed to a discipline of spiritual growth that includes more than table grace (for example, daily prayer, Bible reading, conversation about faith, theological reading, lifestyle adjustments, innovation and experimentation)? **(SF)**

    Staff perspective ___

34. **(53)** Do congregational leaders understand themselves to be *called into a ministry* or *recruited to do a task*? (**Note:** Record the *average score* on a 1-10 scale with 1 signifying "task only" and 10 signifying "call only.") **(PF, SF)**

    Staff perspective ___

35. **(54)** Are congregational leaders perceived to be *anxious* or *open* about creative new ideas? (**Note:** Record the *average score* on a 1-10 scale with 1 signifying "very anxious" and 10 signifying "very open.")

    Staff perspective ___

36. **(55)** Are congregational leaders perceived to be *fearful* or *daring* about taking a stand on controversial issues? (**Note:** Record the *average score* on a 1-10 scale with 1 signifying "very fearful" and 10 signifying "very daring.")

    Staff perspective ___

37. **(58)** How do congregational leaders intentionally listen to marginal members and the spiritually yearning, institutionally alienated public?

38. **(60)** How do staff members help others discern their own calling or ministry? (**Note:** Include a response from both program *and* support staff. Focus on deliberate disciplines or repeatable methods.)

    How the *pastor* does it:

    How the *program staff* do it:

    How the *support staff* do it:

Equipping Disciples:

39. **(62)** How much money is dedicated to training staff?

Total Budget	Amount for staff continuing education	% of total budget

40. **(63)** List the training opportunities for small and large group leaders.

Training opportunity	How often during the year	Who leads it?

41. **(64)** List the training opportunities for program leaders and mission teams.

Training opportunity	How often during the year	Who leads it?

42. **(65)** List the training opportunities for church members to share faith with friends, relatives, work associates, and neighbors.

Training opportunity	How often during the year	Who leads it?

43. **(66)** How do social service missions by the congregation communicate their faith motivation to the general public?

44. **(67)** How does the congregation train volunteers to work sensitively with other cultures, ethnic groups, or minorities in their local community or global partnerships?

45. **(68)** How does the congregation recognize, commission, and prayerfully support emerging mission volunteers?

46. **(69)** Who monitors volunteer performance and targets appropriate standards of quality?

47. **(70)** How much time and energy does the pastor give to empowering lay ministries? (**Note:** Record the *average score* on a 1-10 scale as indicated below.)

	Is the pastor doing ministry alone (1) or mentoring apprentices to do that ministry (10)?	Is the pastor doing tasks on behalf of the church (1) or training others to do the same work (10)?	Is the pastor counseling with individuals (1) or coaching in groups (10)?
Staff persective			

Deploying Servants:

48. **(71)** List all of the missions and ministries related to your congregation, and see how church members related to them. **(GT, CC, AJ)**

Mission or Ministry	Property use only (free use or rental)	Financial support only	Church members set policy	Church members participate in the mission	Approximate # of church members involved	Staff or church leaders involved

49. **(74)** Does worship regularly focus prayer or celebration on one or more of the missions or ministries listed in question 48?

Form

Finance:

50. **(97)** Compare the *average weekly* giving of members and leaders.

Average staff giving: ____

Communication:

51. **(102)** What are the membership trends for the past ten years? **(PF, EH)**

	Total members beginning year	**Removed by death**	**Removed by transfer or other means**	**Received by affirmation of faith**	**Received by transfer or other means**	**Total members year end**
Current year						
Last year						
Two years ago						
Three years ago						
Four years ago						
Five years ago						
Six years ago						
Seven years ago						
Eight years ago						
Nine years ago						

52. **(103)** What media is used to communicate within and beyond the church? **(LP)**

	Within the church	**Beyond the church**
Direct mail		
Door-to-door visitation		
Newsletters		
Videotapes		
Sunday announcements		
Bulletin inserts or handouts		
Computer networks		
Posters		
Cable television		
Newspapers		
Radio		
Billboard, bus, park bench advertising		
Other		

53. **(105)** How are editors, producers, or other leaders of communication networks selected and trained?

54. **(106)** List the mission partners with whom the congregation interacts regularly.

	Mission Partners	**Is there an interactive display visible in the foyer or fellowship center?**
Global		
Ecumenical		
Denominational		
Interfaith		
Corporate		
Government		
Social Service		

55. *(***107***)* Are designated staff or laity equipped to relate to segments of the public in the appropriate languages and cultural forms?

THE CONGREGATIONAL MISSION ASSESSMENT

WORSHIP SERVICE SURVEY

Dear Brother or Sister in Christ:

Your church is seeking God's direction for its future ministry and mission. In order to understand the obstacles and opportunities for your church, we need your help.

Please complete this worksheet to the best of your ability. *Do not* sign your name. Other groups are also being asked to complete worksheets. All the information will be compiled to complete a broad, clear picture of your congregational life. An interpretation and recommendations will be shared with the whole congregation.

Thank you very, very much for your help.

In Christ's Service,

Your Congregational Leaders

WORSHIP SERVICE SURVEY

The same worksheet will be distributed at two consecutive worship services. Please complete it each time and feel free to add any new insight or idea. These will be collated and combined with data from other groups. The number in bold parenthesis **(#)** indicates the question number on the master congregational mission assessment form.

1. **(102)** Are you a member of this church?

   Yes ____ **No** ____

2. **(2)** How did you start attending this church?

   - As a result of a particular mission or ministry of the church ___
   - As a result of an invitation from a member ___
   - By choosing this church out of several I visited ___
   - By growing up in this church ___

3. **(41)** How far do you drive?

	less than a mile	**1 – 3 miles**	**4 – 6 miles**	**7 –9 miles**	**10 – 15 miles**	**more than 15 miles**
To work						
To shop						
To church						

4. **(44)** If you are a parent, is the nursery meeting your expectations? **Place the appropriate number in the corresponding space below.**

   Poor! *1 2 3 4 5 6 7 8 9 10* **Perfect!**

   Sufficient cribs ___
   Space for toddlers ___
   Separation of infants and toddlers ___
   Accessibility ___
   Security ___
   Light, heat, and water ___
   Staffing ___
   Equipment ___

5. **(4)** How welcome and included do you feel in this church? **Circle the number on the scale from 1-10 that best measures your experience.**

   I still feel like an outsider! *1 2 3 4 5 6 7 8 9 10* **They took me right into their hearts!**

6. **(3)** What are your preferences in music, television, and reading?

   Radio:

   Country ___
   Christian ___
   "Oldies" ___
   Soft Rock ___
   Hard Rock ___
   Rap ___
   Classical ___
   News/Talk ___
   Public Radio ___

Television:	Daytime Soaps ___	Game Shows ___	Movie: Comedy ___
	Daytime Reruns ___	Sports ___	Movie: Drama ___
	Sitcoms ___	News ___	Movie: Action ___
	Talk Shows ___	Educational ___	Other ___

What is your favorite television show? ______________________

Magazine:	Current Events ___	Transportation ___	Sports ___
	Special Interest ___	Educational ___	Home and Garden ___

What is your favorite magazine? __________________________

7. **(33)** What is the most important benefit you receive from this worship service? **Check one or more.**

I feel changed and different!	I feel cared for and supported!	I feel motivated to serve and learn all week!	I learn important information and insights!	I am connected to mission—locally and globally!

Which worship service do you attend?

8. **(40)** How do you rate your worship leadership? **Place the appropriate number in the corresponding box below.**

Poor! *1 2 3 4 5 6 7 8 9 10* **Perfect!**

Leader(s)	Sincerity	Spiritual depth	Skills	Approachability and friendliness	Team cooperation
Preacher					
Organist					
Liturgists					
Band musicians					
Choir members					
Greeters					
Ushers					
Others					

9. **(72)** Do you participate regularly in a particular mission or ministry of your congregation?

   Yes ___ **No** ___

10. **(97)** My *average weekly* gift to the church is: $______

11. **(38)** What is your most memorable experience (positive or negative) from worship services in the past year?

What happened?	Why was it so memorable?

12. **(48)** Rate the quality of *volunteer(lay)* leadership for nurturing personal, relational, and spiritual growth that you have personally experienced. **Circle the most appropriate number.**

Poor! *1 2 3 4 5 6 7 8 9 10* **Perfect!**

13. **(49)** Rate the quality of *pastoral l*eadership for nurturing personal, relational, and spiritual growth that you personally have experienced. **Circle the most appropriate number.**

Poor! *1 2 3 4 5 6 7 8 9 10* **Perfect!**

14. **(50)** Think of a time of crisis or confusion during your life. What person within the church helped you resolve or overcome it?

Time of crisis	**The person in the church who helped me**

15. **(51)** Do you have a specific spiritual practice (in addition to table grace) that you exercise through the week (including daily prayer, Bible reading, conversation about faith, theological reading)?

Yes ___ **No** ___

16. **(59)** Does participation in congregational life influence your lifestyle and career? **Circle the most appropriate number.**

Not at all! *1 2 3 4 5 6 7 8 9 10* **Overwhelming influence!**

17. **(53)** Do you think most of your congregational volunteer leaders believe they are c*alled by God to a ministry* or *recruited by the church to do a task*? **Circle the most appropriate number.**

Just a job! *1 2 3 4 5 6 7 8 9 10* **Called by God!**

18. **(54)** Do you think most of your congregational leaders (volunteer and staff) are *anxious* about, or *open* to creative new ideas? **Circle the most appropriate number.**

Very anxious! *1 2 3 4 5 6 7 8 9 10* **Really open!**

19. **(55)** Do you think most of your congregational leaders (volunteers and staff) are *fearful* or *daring* about taking stands on controversial issues? **Circle the most appropriate number.**

Very fearful! *1 2 3 4 5 6 7 8 9 10* **Positively daring!**

20. **(12)** Based on your understanding of the identity of your congregation, does your pastor model the values, beliefs, vision, and mission of the congregation? **Circle the most appropriate number.**

No, not at all! *1 2 3 4 5 6 7 8 9 10* **Yes, completely!**

21. **(13)** Does your official body of elected officers model the values, beliefs, vision, and mission of the congregation? **Circle the most appropriate number.**

No, not at all! *1 2 3 4 5 6 7 8 9 10* **Yes, completely!**

22. **(14)** Do the core leaders of various groups and programs model the values, beliefs, vision, and mission of the congregation? **Circle the most appropriate number.**

No, not at all! *1 2 3 4 5 6 7 8 9 10* **Yes, completely!**

23. **(108)** How well does your church secretary interact with the public? **Circle the most appropriate number.**

Poor! *1 2 3 4 5 6 7 8 9 10* **Perfect!**

24. **(15)** Where do you think the pastor invests his or her time and energy?

	% of energy on church members	**% of energy on non-members**	**% of energy on personal growth**	**% of energy on denominational duties**	**% of energy on other personal and family issues**
Your perspective					

25. **(16)** Where do you think core leaders invest their time and energy?

Program Area	**% of energy on church members**	**% of energy on non-members**	**% of energy on personal growth**	**% of energy on denominational duties**	**% of energy on other personal and family issues**
Worship					
Education					
Visitation					

26. **(70)** How much time and energy do you think your pastor gives to empowering volunteer ministries? **Place the appropriate number, between 1 and 10, in the boxes below.**

	Is the pastor doing ministry alone (1) or mentoring apprentices to do that ministry (10)?	**Is the pastor doing tasks on behalf of the church (1) or training others to do the same work (10)?**	**Is the pastor counseling with individuals (1) or coaching in groups (10)?**
Your perspective			

27. **(30)** Do you consider the pastor to be a leader? **Choose an appropriate number between 1, being not at all, and 10, being absolutely**.

	Causes things to happen.	***Really gets people moving.***	***Sees deep and far.***	***Takes risks and experiments with new ideas.***	***Builds bridges between opposite views and diverse ideas.***
Your perspective					

28. **(81)** Do you think trustees and property managers understand their job as *maintenance of church assets* or *the resourcing of congregational mission*? **Circle the most appropriate number.**

Maintain the property and preserve status quo! *1 2 3 4 5 6 7 8 9 10* **Do whatever it takes to create a launching pad for mission!**

29. **(91)** Do you think the treasurers and financial managers understand their job as *the maintenance of church assets* or *the resourcing of congregational mission*? **Circle the most appropriate number.**

Save the money for a rainy day! *1 2 3 4 5 6 7 8 9 10* **Give it all away to maximize creative mission!**

30. **(100)** When the church asks you for money, do you think it is primarily intended to *keep the doors open* or *open new doors*? **Circle the most appropriate number.**

Keep the doors open! *1 2 3 4 5 6 7 8 9 10* **Open new doors!**

31. **(22)** Remember or imagine any creative new mission idea the church has implemented or might implement in the future. Without reference to any official diagram of church structure, describe or draw how that idea would be approved and implemented.

32. **(110)** Please add anything you think might be helpful to your congregational leaders as they think about the future of this church.

Thank you for taking the time to help us!

THE CONGREGATIONAL MISSION ASSESSMENT

RANDOM CONGREGATIONAL SURVEY

Dear Brother or Sister in Christ:

Your church is seeking God's direction for its future ministry and mission. In order to understand the obstacles and opportunities for your church, we need your help.

Please complete this worksheet to the best of your ability. *Do not* sign your name. Other groups are also being asked to complete worksheets. All the information will be compiled to complete a broad, clear picture of your congregational life. An interpretation and recommendations will be shared with the whole congregation.

Thank you very, very much for your help.

In Christ's Service,

Your Congregational Leaders

RANDOM CONGREGATIONAL SURVEY

Please complete this worksheet to the best of your ability. These responses will be collated and combined with data from other groups.

1. **(102)** Are you a member of this church?

   Yes ____ **No** ____

2. **(2)** How did you start attending this church?

   - As a result of a particular mission or ministry of the church ___
   - As a result of an invitation from a member ___
   - By choosing this church out of several visited ___
   - By growing up in this church ___

3. **(4)** How welcome and included do you feel in this church? **Circle the number on the scale from 1-10 that best measures your experience.**

   I still feel like an outsider! *1 2 3 4 5 6 7 8 9 10* **They took me right into their hearts!**

4. **(32)** Looking back on last year, I think I attended worship with the following regularity. **Indicate for each month if you think you attended 1, 2, 3, 4, or more times.**

Jan ___	Feb ___	Mar ___	Apr ___	May ___	June ___
July ___	Aug ___	Sept ___	Oct ___	Nov ___	Dec ____

5. **(41)** How far do you drive?

	less than a mile	**1 – 3 miles**	**4 – 6 miles**	**7 –9 miles**	**10 – 15 miles**	**more than 15 miles**
To work						
To shop						
To church						

6. **(3)** What are your preferences in music, television, and reading?

Radio:	Country	___	Soft Rock	___	Classical	___
	Christian	___	Hard Rock	___	News/Talk	___
	"Oldies"	___	Rap	___	Public Radio	___
Television:	Daytime Soaps	___	Game Shows	___	Movie: Comedy	___
	Daytime Reruns	___	Sports	___	Movie: Drama	___
	Sitcoms	___	News	___	Movie: Action	___
	Talk Shows	___	Educational	___	Other	___

What is your favorite television show? ________________________

Magazine:	Current Events ___	Transportation ___	Sports ___
	Special Interest ___	Educational ___	Home and Garden ___

What is your favorite magazine? ________________________________

7. **(44)** If you are a parent, is the nursery meeting your expectations? **Place the appropriate number in the corresponding space below.**

Poor! *1 2 3 4 5 6 7 8 9 10* **Perfect!**

Sufficient cribs	___	Security	___
Space for toddlers	___	Light, heat, and water	___
Separation of infants and toddlers	___	Staffing	___
Accessibility	___	Equipment	___

8. **(33)** What is the most important benefit you receive from this worship service? **Check one or more.**

I feel changed and different!	**I feel cared for and supported!**	**I feel motivated to serve and learn all week!**	**I learn important information and insights!**	**I am connected to mission—locally and globally!**
Which worship service do you attend?				

9. **(40)** How do you rate your worship leadership? **Place the appropriate number in the corresponding box below.**

Poor! *1 2 3 4 5 6 7 8 9 10* **Perfect!**

Leader(s)	**Sincerity**	**Spiritual depth**	**Skills**	**Approachability and friendliness**	**Team cooperation**
Preacher					
Organist					
Liturgists					
Band musicians					
Choir members					
Greeters					
Ushers					
Others					

10. **(48)** Rate the quality of *volunteer (lay)* leadership for nurturing personal, relational, and spiritual growth that you have personally experienced. **Circle the most appropriate number.**

Poor! *1 2 3 4 5 6 7 8 9 10* **Perfect!**

11. **(49)** Rate the quality of *pastoral* leadership for nurturing personal, relational, and spiritual growth that you have experienced. **Circle the most appropriate number.**

Poor! *1 2 3 4 5 6 7 8 9 10* **Perfect!**

12. **(51)** Do you have a specific spiritual practice (in addition to table grace) that you exercise through the week (including daily prayer, Bible reading, conversation about faith, theological reading)?

Yes ___ **No** ___

13. **(59)** Does participation in congregational life influence your lifestyle and career? **Circle the most appropriate number.**

Not at all! *1 2 3 4 5 6 7 8 9 10* **Overwhelming influence!**

14. **(12)** Based on your understanding of the identity of your congregation, does your pastor model the values, beliefs, vision, and mission of the congregation? **Circle the most appropriate number.**

No, not at all! *1 2 3 4 5 6 7 8 9 10* **Yes, completely!**

15. **(13)** Do your core leaders of groups and programs model the values, beliefs, vision, and mission of the congregation? **Circle the most appropriate number.**

No, not at all! *1 2 3 4 5 6 7 8 9 10* **Yes, completely!**

16. **(108)** How well does your church secretary interact with the public? **Place the appropriate number in the corresponding box below.**

Poor! *1 2 3 4 5 6 7 8 9 10* **Perfect!**

17. **(70)** How much time and energy do you think your pastor gives to empowering volunteer ministries? **Place the appropriate number between 1 and 10 in the boxes below.**

	Is the pastor doing ministry alone (1) or mentoring apprentices to do that ministry (10)?	**Is the pastor doing tasks on behalf of the church (1) or training others to do the same work (10)?**	**Is the pastor counseling with individuals (1) or coaching in groups (10)?**
Your perspective			

18. **(81)** Do you think trustees and property managers understand their job as *the maintenance of church assets* or *the resourcing of congregational mission*? **Circle the most appropriate number.**

Maintain the property and preserve status quo! *1 2 3 4 5 6 7 8 9 10* **Do whatever it takes to make a launching pad for mission!**

19. **(91)** Do you think the treasurers and financial managers understand their job as *the maintenance of church assets* or *the resourcing of congregational mission*? **Circle the most appropriate number.**

Save the money for a rainy day! *1 2 3 4 5 6 7 8 9 10* **Give it all away to maximize creative mission!**

20. **(100)** When the church asks you for money, do you think it is primarily intended to *keep the doors open* or *open new doors*? **Circle the most appropriate number.**

Keep the doors open! *1 2 3 4 5 6 7 8 9 10* **Open new doors!**

21. **(110)** Please add anything you think will be helpful to your congregational leaders as they think about the future of this church.

Thank you for taking the time to help us!

A GUIDE TO DEMOGRAPHIC RESEARCH

A GUIDE TO THE MOST HELPFUL INFORMATION FOR CONGREGATIONAL PLANNING

The following guide identifies nine basic categories of information, with no more than five questions in each category. Following each category is a brief tip explaining why the information will be useful. When you do demographic research be aware of these three cautions:

1) Be sure to study your own identity and the community context together. Gather your data in parallel columns so that you can compare and contrast the results.

2) If you are considering the viability of your congregation, be sure to make a distinction between the viability of the institution of the church as a community organization and the mission of the church as a spiritual organization.

3) Do not leap to any decisions about programs, staff, or budget until you have completed the full assessment.

If you heed these cautions, you will find that this research can help you plan your future with confidence in your ability and with motivation to implement your plans.

Congregations in the United States can obtain civic demographic information through private companies such as Percept (151 Kalmus Drive, Suite A104, Costa Mesa, CA 92626-5900). You can reach Percept at 1-800-442-6277 or by fax at 1-714-957-1924). Denominational offices are increasingly becoming adept at providing demographic information. One of the better agencies is Research Services, Presbyterian Church (U.S.A.), 100 Witherspoon Street, Louisville, Kentucky 40202; the phone number is 1-800-997-8934.

You can also obtain information free directly from the United States Census Bureau Web site (www.census.gov). Once on the Web site, click on the "search" button. Then select "place search" from the search options. On the next screen, type the zip code(s) or the name(s) of the place(s) you wish to review. Browse using keywords, maps, or census tables. There are currently more than three hundred variables from which to choose, and the information here can guide you in your choices. Once submitted, you will need to identify the format in which you wish to download the results.

Congregations in Canada are hindered by the fact that there is no nationwide company that can provide this service for churches. Denominational offices are not yet fully equipped to give you the total information you wish. Some helpful information can be obtained for a fee from the corporate research company Environics Research Group Ltd., 45 Charles Street East, Toronto, ON M4Y 1S2 (phone 416-964-1397, fax 416-964-2486).

The federal agency Statistics Canada only surveys religious information every eight years (the 2000 census is the most recent). It is very helpful for obtaining data gathered in 1996 and 1992 in order to trace general societal trends. On the other hand, Statistics Canada offers a variety of E-Pubs that can be downloaded from their Web site (www.statcan.ca) or ordered by calling 1-800-263-1136. Two years after the census, the government publishes a yearbook with excellent summaries of demographic and psychographic trends using information from the Canadian census and surveys from various Canadian health and education agencies. For a fee you can specify the information within a fifteen-kilometer radius of your church that you wish to attain. You can order the information by phone 1-800-267-6677 or 1-800-263-1136, fax 1-800-889-9734, or e-mail order@statcan.ca. The postal address is Statistics Canada, Dissemination Division, 120 Parkdale Avenue, Ottawa, Ontario K1A 0T6.

Canadians think more regionally than Americans, so you can gather further demographic information by contacting regional reference centers:

Atlantic Region (including Newfoundland)
Advisory Services
1741 Brunswick Street
2nd Floor, Box 11
Halifax, NS B3J 3X8
Phone: 902-426-5331
Fax: 902-426-9538

Prairie Region
Saskatchewan:
Advisory Services
Park Plaza, Suite 440
2365 Albert Street
Regina, SK S4P 4K1
Phone: 306-780-5405
Fax: 306-780-5403

Manitoba:
Advisory Services
Via Rail Building, Suite 200
123 Main Street
Winnipeg, Manitoba R3C 4V9
Phone: 204-983-4020
Fax: 204-983-7543

Northern Alberta and the Northwest Territories:
Advisory Services
Park Square, 9th Floor
10001 Bellamy Hill
Edmonton, AL T5J 3B6
Phone: 403-495-3027
Fax: 403-495-5318

Southern Alberta:
Advisory Services
Discovery Place, Room 201
3553-31 Street N.W.
Calgary, AL T2L 2K7
Phone: 403-292-6717
Fax: 403-292-4958

Quebec Region
Advisory Services
200 René Levesque Boulevard West
Guy Favreau Complex
4th Floor, East Tower
Montreal, Quebec H2Z 1X4
Phone: 514-283-5725
Fax: 514-283-9350

Ontario Region
Advisory Services
Arthur Meighen Building, 10th Floor
25 St. Clair Avenue East
Toronto, ON M4T 1M4
Phone: 416-973-6586
Fax: 416-973-7475

National Capitol Region
Statistics Reference Centre
R. H. Coats Building, Lobby
Holland Avenue
Ottawa, ON K1A 0T6
Phone: 613-951-8116
Fax: 613-951-0581

Pacific Region (including Yukon Territory)
Advisory Services
Liberty Square Office Tower
600-300 West Georgia Street
Vancouver, BC V6B 6C7
Phone: 604-666-3691
Fax: 604-666-4863

Question 1 in the congregational mission assessment tool invites you to use the following chart to compare data about your community with data about your congregation.

Birth Years

Line		1966–1985 % of congregation	1946–1965 % of congregation	1936–1945 % of congregation	1915–1935 % of congregation	1900–1914 % of congregation
1	**Total % in this age group**					

Demographic Diversity

Line		% of adult worshipers		Line		% of adult worshipers
				7	**Household Income:** Under $10,000	
1	**Married**				$10,000–29,999	
2	**Divorced/Separated**				$30,000–49,999	
3	**Widowed**				$50,000–69,999	
4	**Never married**				$70,000–89,999	
					Over $90,000	
5	**Households with children at home**					
				8	**Homeowners**	
				9	**Renters**	
6	**Cultural Background:** Western European				**Education:** Below high school	
	Eastern European				High school	
	African				College/University	
	Hispanic				Career training	
	Caribbean				Advanced degree	
	Asian					
	Pacific Rim			10	**Technology Use:**	
	Middle Eastern				Cell phone	
	Far Eastern				Computer	
	Native North American				Internet	
					Microwave	

This chart represents the minimum information you should gather, but I urge you to gather as much information as you can in the following categories. Many of these statistics can be easily illustrated in charts or graphs that will aid in the presentation of your recommendations to the congregation.

Age:

The best way to group ages is by birth year. Generally speaking, people born before 1945 are known as the "Builder" generation. Those born between 1945 and 1965 are the "Boomer" generation. Those born between 1966 and 1985 are the "Buster" generation. Those born after 1985 are the emerging "Echo" generation. The exact dates vary when applied to these generations, because what marks these groupings of people is not age as much as attitude and lifestyle. If you wish, break down the age groups into smaller categories. There are many books that can help you interpret the attitudes and lifestyles of these generations in the context of your ministry. Once you have discerned the spread of ages represented in your church, answer the following key questions:

a) What is the median age of your congregational membership?
b) What is the median age of participants in worship?
c) What is the average age of congregational leadership?

This information will help you identify which generations present in the community are present or missing from congregational participation. It will help you better understand why your worship liturgies and music are or are not effective in inviting the participation of each generation. Further reflection on the lifestyles and attitudes of each generation will guide you in developing programs that can touch these generations in both style and content.

Marriage and Family:

In this time of mobility and diversity, personal relationships are more important than ever. At any given time, at least half of the public is single, and many are disconnected with family life. Peer groups and work associates are often more influential than immediate family in shaping our behavior and attitudes. People are seeking to recover from broken relationships or build new, healthy relationships. Your research should allow you to answer these questions:

a) What percent of people in your community and congregation are married, separated, divorced, widowed, or have never been married?
b) What percent of the households in the community and congregation require both parents to earn incomes to maintain the family?
c) What percent of the households in the community and congregation have young children at home during the workday?

This information will help you understand the patterns of relationship that influence behavior in your congregation and community. It can help you focus ministries to address relational issues and give you a sense of priority for child care or elder care opportunities. Combined with reflection about lifestyle, attitude, and spiritual calling, it will help you customize worship options and develop small group ministry options.

Household Income and Home Ownership:

The gap between rich and poor is widening, and income largely determines future opportunities for family growth, education, leisure, medical care, and career potential. Home ownership has become a key to both self-esteem and future opportunity. Since it really is true that "you get what you pay for," it is important to discover the real financial resources of the community and congregation. Since it is also true that people spend money for what they really value, it is important to contrast congregational giving to the church with community giving to charity. Your research should answer these questions:

a) What is the average income of households in your congregation and community?
b) What is the average, annual charitable giving of households in your congregation and community?
c) What percent of the congregation and community own their own home?

This information will help you identify what your real income potential might be as a church if people were truly motivated to give. it may also give you insight into the real debt burdens church members bear and the priorities they have in spending money. Further reflection on lifestyles and economics can help you design stewardship or mission programs and guide you in determining reasonable goals for major capital fund raising.

Cultural Background and Ethnicity:

Cultural diversity is the most significant issue emerging in church growth in the twenty-first century. We are experiencing population shifts due to immigration as never before. This is influencing small towns and villages, just as it is changing urban centers. Many churches live such insular lives that they are quite unaware of the changes in language, lifestyle, shopping, and leisure activities resulting from a changing cultural mix in the community. Your research should answer these questions:

a) What cultural or ethnic groups are represented in your congregation and community?
b) What cultures are represented in and what languages are spoken by your congregational staff and community?
c) What patterns in congregation and community are emerging between cultural orientation, income, and church participation?

Not only will this information help you discern which cultural groups could be expected to be present but are missing from your congregation, but also this information can help you anticipate the language, program, and lifestyle issues that will need to be addressed for effective future ministry. This can guide you in future conversations with community partners, in customizing future outreach programs, and in future staff acquisition and deployment.

Education:

Education is a measure of three things that are significant to the church. It indicates the direction of specialized knowledge that congregational participants can be assumed to have. It indicates the breadth of awareness congregational participants can be expected to demonstrate. It indicates the commitment congregational participants may have to rational or reflective problem solving. With your research, you should be able to answer the following questions:

a) What percent of our congregation and community can be assumed to bring a broad, liberal arts background to their interpretation of global and personal experience?
b) What percent of our congregation and community have very specialized educational backgrounds, and what kinds of expertise do they bring to potential ministries?
c) What percent of our congregation and community share a high priority for continuing education, and what kinds of skills will they deem most important?

This information will help you understand how you can best communicate with different segments of the congregation and community. It will shape preaching, music programs, marketing strategies, and crisis intervention tactics. It will help you form realistic continuing education targets, topics, and learning processes.

Technologies, Occupations, and Skills:

Technology has emerged today as a leading indicator of readiness for personal, spiritual, and professional growth. The technologies of home, leisure, and work have merged into a seamless interdependency. The challenge is not just for the church to empower participants to use the most up-to-date professional skills for ministry, but to merge ministry into the seamless fabric of home, work, and leisure activities of the people. With your research, you should be able to answer the following questions:

a) What communication technologies are people in your congregation and community most familiar with?
b) What interactive learning technologies are people in your church and community most comfortable with?
c) What occupations do people in your congregation and community have, and what kinds of special skills do they need to do their work?

This information not only gives you an idea of the talents available to the congregation, but it allows you to discern how leadership can best be networked for effective ministries. You will be able to customize Christian education and anticipate gaps in skill or technology that may hinder future outreach. Finally, you will better understand the diverse attitudes, lifestyles, and personal expectations of congregational participants.

Geography:

Although church members reside in a particular locality, they are often unaware of policies and long-term plans related to zoning bylaws, environmental protection, housing development, transportation corridors, and other matters. Local and municipal planners have information about the future of the area that is crucial to your strategic plans. Your research should be able to answer the following questions:

a) What is the average cost of property in your community or region?
b) What is the real market value of your church property?
c) What zoning restrictions does the municipality place on your property development?
d) What areas of the municipality have been marked for significant population growth?
e) Where will the most significant places people will gather in the next ten years be?

This information is important for the renovation of existing property and for the location of future mission properties. Your church can anticipate whether it will be at the center or at the margins of community development, and your church can make wise decisions to invest in land acquisition. This data will help you complete the last three sub-systems of the congregational mission assessment tool, which are related to property, finance, and communication.

Mobility:

Church leaders tend to experience personal stability in their own lives, so they may not appreciate the mobility in the lives of others. This information effects your expectations for leadership development and stewardship, and perhaps more important, it influences public expectations of what the church should offer. Here are the questions you need to answer:

a) How frequently do people move in and out of the community?
b) What is the average distance people drive to work, to shop, and to worship?
c) How many passengers are usually transported by car to the church?
d) How do people expect to "get around" in their community?

This information will help you estimate the continuity of financial support that you can expect in major capital building campaigns or creative mission projects. It will also help you understand people's reluctance to maintain the heritage of a particular church, their sense of grief for people and cultures left behind, and their particular yearning for intimacy and hope in the place they now live. Understanding mobility will help you design spirituality to be more relevant and portable. This will inform your answers to questions from the middle, "functional" sub-systems of the congregational mission assessment tool.

Aesthetic Taste and Lifestyle:

This kind of data is sometimes described as "psychographics" because it measures less tangible attitudes and personal preferences. Question 3 in the assessment tool, for example, asks people to identify their favorite music, television program, or magazine. Preferences in automobiles, architecture, vacation plans, and fashion are also important measurements of attitude. All of these choices reveal how people come to discover meaning in their lives. Automobile dealers and restaurant franchises often have elaborate psychographic information about a given community. This information should answer these questions:

a) What kind of music, television programs, and magazines do people in the congregation and community enjoy?
b) What kind of automobiles are people in the congregation and community most likely to drive?
c) What kind of dress, jewelry, or body ornamentation are people likely to display?
d) What kinds of stores do people shop in, and what kinds of groceries do they buy?

Such information is important to the church as it trues to connect with the diverse public in the community. This will guide your hospitality strategy as you welcome people and offer refreshments. It will influence the choice and behavioral expectations of clergy and lay leadership. This data will inform your answers to the identity questions of the congregational mission assessment tool.

Religion:

Churches need to be aware of the other organizations, agencies, and corporations that are active in the community. This is not primarily to identify competition, but to discern potential partnerships. Much of the local and global mission today is too complex and too costly to accomplish alone. You will need to discover partners who are compatible with your own identity and can help you carry out mission.

a) What Christian groups (churches, para-churches, informal networks) are active in your community?
b) What Christian partnerships (clergy associations, ecumenical organizations) are active in your community?
c) What other religious faiths (mainstream, new age, cultic) are active in your community?
d) What percentage of the population is *not* attached to any religion at all?

This information will help you understand the diversity of meaning and symbolism in your community and give some indication as to the ferment of seeking that is alive among the people. Such information can shape your conversation or marketing strategies and guide the congregation to assess potential partners in ministry. Such data will help you complete the organizational and leadership questions in the congregational mission assessment tool.

A PROFILE OF OUR CONGREGATION

DEMOGRAPHIC INFORMATION ABOUT OUR CHURCH

Dear Brothers and Sisters in Christ:

Our congregation is committed to offer the best quality and the most relevant ministries to the diverse individuals and groups in our community. We believe God's love is for everyone, and we want to do our best to make sure everyone can experience God's love.

We ask individual congregational participants—*18 years old or over*—to complete this brief survey. Similar information is being gathered to help us understand the diversity of the community in which we live. This information will help us design effective ministries in the future.

Please *do not* provide your name or address. This information is confidential, and will not be released for any use whatsoever beyond our congregational mission.

Thank you very much for your help. Please continue to pray for our church as we follow Christ into new and renewed ministry in the twenty-first century.

Faithfully,

Your Congregational Leaders

OUR CONGREGATIONAL RESEARCH

Your name is *not* requested.

If you participate in any way in our congregation, and are *at least 18 years old*, please complete the following survey and return it personally or by mail to the church office. *Thank you* for helping our church design ministries that share God's love in the most relevant way to all the people of our community.

1) This is my relationship to this church (check as many as apply):

   ___ I am a participant in the congregation.
   ___ I am a member of the church.
   ___ I am an elected or appointed officer or leader in the church.

2) I have participated in some way in the life of this congregation for:

   ___ more than 20 years
   ___ 15–20 years
   ___ 10–15 years
   ___ 5–10 years
   ___ 1–5 years
   ___ less than 1 year

3) I was born between the following years:

   ___ 1900–1924 ___ 1925–1945 ___ 1946–1964 ___ 1965–1982

4) My current relational status is:

   ___ single, never married ___ married ___ separated or divorced

5) My cultural background is:

   ___ Western European
   ___ Caribbean
   ___ Native North American
   ___ Eastern European
   ___ Asian
   ___ Middle Eastern
   ___ African
   ___ Pacific Rim
   ___ Far Eastern

6) Other than English, I read or speak the following languages:

   ___ Spanish
   ___ Korean
   ___ French
   ___ Chinese
   ___ Creole
   ___ Japanese
   Other: ________________

7) My education background is:

   ___ below high school
   ___ college or university
   ___ high school
   ___ career or professional training

8) I regularly travel the following distances to work, shop, or worship:

	Less than 1 mile	1–5 miles	6–10 miles	10–15 miles	More than 15 miles
to work					
to shop					
to worship					

9) I live in:

___ an apartment
___ a condominium
___ a single, detached house
___ a town house or link home
___ other

10) I have lived in my current location for:

___ less than 1 year
___ 1–3 years
___ 4–7 years
___ 8–10 years
___ 10–15 years
___ more than 15 years

11) My occupation is in the following area:

___ Business, finance, and administration
___ Sales and services
___ Health
___ Education
___ Agriculture
___ Construction
___ Corporate management
___ Trades, transport, and equipment
___ Social service
___ Natural and applied sciences
___ Accommodation and food services
___ Government services

Other: ____

12) My current *household* annual income is:

___ under $10,000
___ $10,000 – $19,999
___ $20,000 – $29,999
___ $30,000 – $39,999
___ $40,000 – $49,999
___ $50,000 – $59,999
___ $60,000 – $69,999
___ $70,000 – $79,999
___ $80,000 – $89,999
___ $90,000 – $99,999
___ over $100,000
___ over $200,000

13) Other than my present church participation, I have participated in the following religious groups:

Other Christian churches: ______________________________

Other faiths: ______________________________

Informal spiritual networks and small groups: ______________________________

14) The music I normally prefer to hear is:

___ Country
___ Christian
___ New Age
___ Soft Rock
___ Hard Rock
___ Rap
___ Classical
___ "Oldies"
___ Jazz

Other: ______________________________

15) The car I drive is:

	North American	**Imported**
Manufacturer:	___ Ford	___ European
	___ GM	___ Japanese or Korean
	___ Other	___ Other
Model:	___ Sedan	___ Sports car
	___ Station wagon	___ Sport utility
	___ Van	___ Truck
Age:	___ less than 1 year old	___ 3 – 6 years old
	___ 1 – 3 years old	___ more than 6 years old

THE LEADERSHIP READINESS TEST

SUMMARY WORKSHEET

Are you ready for change? Is the leadership of your congregation, both staff and volunteer, ready to lead change? Church growth will require adjustments in attitude, shifts in time management, training in new skills, and high trust and cooperation. Both the staff and official body are asked to respond to the following statements by identifying their relative personal agreement on a scale of 1 to 10. These responses will be averaged for the staff and the official body. The averages will be compared to each other, and to the average responses from more than two hundred congregations across North America.

Generally, lower scores indicate more readiness to do whatever it takes to grow, reach out, and address the needs of the unchurched public. Higher scores indicate that leaders are less ready to change attitudes, prioritize time, acquire skills, or let go of control. If scores are high, the congregation will move more slowly, with more stress, and require the coaching or replacing of leaders. An average score over 4.0 suggests that the congregation will find it very difficult to reach out to the unchurched without a major change in attitude and openness. Scores in the second column are the average of two hundred churches in North America. (**Note:** All churches score higher on questions 6, 7, and 8 than on all of the other questions.)

Total Agreement *1 2 3 4 5 6 7 8 9 10* **Total Disagreement**

	Our Official Body	Average Official Body
1. The nursery should be extra clean, neat, staffed with paid help, and open every time there is a church function.	____	2.86
2. Turf issues are harmful to the growth of a church.	____	2.95
3. I am willing for the facilities to be used even if they get dirty.	____	2.48
4. Reaching out to new members is just as important as taking care of the present members.	____	1.94
5. I am comfortable with radical change if it will help my church reach more people for Christ.	____	3.34
6. I am seldom concerned about procedure.	____	5.08
7. Paying off the debt is a major concern to me.	____	5.46
8. Let's spend some of the financial reserves to hire more staff or start new programs.	____	4.93

9. Several worship services are fine with me because I am more interested in meeting the needs of all the people than I am in knowing everyone at church.	____	2.42
10. I am not offended when my pastor (team) does not give me regular personal attention.	____	2.40
11. I realize that more staff is needed today than in the past.	____	2.35
12. I trust and affirm my pastor's (team's) efforts to reach more people for Christ.	____	1.96

	Our Staff	**Average Staff**
1. The nursery should be extra clean, neat, staffed with paid help, and open every time there is a church function.	____	2.02
2. Turf issues are harmful to the growth of a church.	____	2.44
3. I am willing for the facilities to be used even if they get dirty.	____	1.84
4. Reaching out to new members is just as important as taking care of the present members.	____	1.83
5. I am comfortable with radical change if it will help my church reach more people for Christ.	____	2.50
6. I am seldom concerned about procedure.	____	4.81
7. Paying off the debt is a major concern to me.	____	4.27
8. Let's spend some of the financial reserves to hire more staff or start new programs.	____	3.21
9. Several worship services are fine with me because I am more interested in meeting the needs of all the people than I am in knowing everyone at church.	____	2.00
10. I am not offended when my pastor (team) does not give me regular personal attention.	____	2.17
11. I realize that more staff is needed today than in the past.	____	1.62
12. I trust and affirm my pastor's (team's) efforts to reach more people for Christ.	____	1.54

(**Note:** The Leadership Readiness Test is also used in *The Complete Ministry Audit* by William Easum, available from Abingdon Press, and can be used to interface these two consultation tools.)

THE LEADERSHIP READINESS TEST

OFFICIAL BODY WORKSHEET

Are you ready for change? Is the leadership of your congregation, both staff and volunteer, ready to lead change? Church growth will require adjustments in attitude, shifts in time management, training in new skills, and high trust and cooperation. Both the staff and official body are asked to respond to the following statements by identifying their relative personal agreement on a scale of 1 to 10. These responses will be averaged for the staff and the official body. The averages will be compared to each other, and to the average responses from more than two hundred congregations across North America.

Total Agreement *1 2 3 4 5 6 7 8 9 10* **Total Disagreement**

1. The nursery should be extra clean, neat, staffed with paid help, and open every time there is a church function. ____
2. Turf issues are harmful to the growth of a church. ____
3. I am willing for the facilities to be used even if they get dirty. ____
4. Reaching out to new members is just as important as taking care of the present members. ____
5. I am comfortable with radical change if it will help my church reach more people for Christ. ____
6. I am seldom concerned about procedure. ____
7. Paying off the debt is a major concern to me. ____
8. Let's spend some of the financial reserves to hire more staff or start new programs. ____
9. Several worship services are fine with me because I am more interested in meeting the needs of all the people than I am in knowing everyone at church. ____
10. I am not offended when my pastor (team) does not give me regular personal attention. ____
11. I realize that more staff is needed today than in the past. ____
12. I trust and affirm my pastor's (team's) efforts to reach more people for Christ. ____

(**Note:** The Leadership Readiness Test is also used in *The Complete Ministry Audit* by William Easum, available from Abingdon Press, and can be used to interface these two consultation tools.)

THE LEADERSHIP READINESS TEST

STAFF WORKSHEET

Are you ready for change? Is the leadership of your congregation, both staff and volunteer, ready to lead change? Church growth will require adjustments in attitude, shifts in time management, training in new skills, and high trust and cooperation. Both the staff and official body are asked to respond to the following statements by identifying their relative personal agreement on a scale of 1 to 10. These responses will be averaged for the staff and the official body. The averages will be compared to each other, and to the average responses from more than two hundred congregations across North America.

Total Agreement *1 2 3 4 5 6 7 8 9 10* **Total Disagreement**

1. The nursery should be extra clean, neat, staffed with paid help, and open every time there is a church function. ____
2. Turf issues are harmful to the growth of a church. ____
3. I am willing for the facilities to be used even if they get dirty. ____
4. Reaching out to new members is just as important as taking care of the present members. ____
5. I am comfortable with radical change if it will help my church reach more people for Christ. ____
6. I am seldom concerned about procedure. ____
7. Paying off the debt is a major concern to me. ____
8. Let's spend some of the financial reserves to hire more staff or start new programs. ____
9. Several worship services are fine with me because I am more interested in meeting the needs of all the people than I am in knowing everyone at church. ____
10. I am not offended when my senior pastor (or team colleagues) do not give me regular personal attention. ____
11. I realize that more staff is needed today than in the past. ____
12. I trust and affirm my senior pastor's (or team colleagues') efforts to reach more people for Christ. ____

(**Note:** The Leadership Readiness Test is also used in *The Complete Ministry Audit* by William Easum, available from Abingdon Press, and can be used to interface these two consultation tools.)

THE CHURCH STRESS TEST

FOR SUMMARY USE

An addiction is an unhealthy behavior pattern that we may deny, but truly undermines our health and blocks productive living. Both individuals *and* organizations can have such unhealthy behavior patterns. When these addictions are pointed out to us, our stress level increases sharply. The following statements are truths that thriving, growing, vital congregations have discovered about mission. These truths are shocking, because they cause us to confront hidden assumptions and addictive behavior patterns that, in the past, have blocked the congregation from growth and mission.

The statements below are admittedly extreme, but they contain a core truth for congregational life in the twenty-first century. Let's see where this congregation will feel the most stress in future change. After each statement, identify your personal level of anxiety by assigning a number between 1 and 10. Responses will be gathered during or after two consecutive worship services and averaged. These results will be combined with all the other information being collected in the *Congregational Mission Assessment.* Turn the page to see the *positive* insights of growing churches!

No Anxiety *1 2 3 4 5 6 7 8 9 10* **High Anxiety**

1. The youth are *not* the future of your church. ______
2. Nobody cares about the *mere* presence of God. ______
3. Every dying church in North America is a friendly congregation. ______
4. There is no such thing as "good" worship. ______
5. Most people don't like organ music. ______
6. It doesn't matter what people retain following the worship service. ______
7. Self-sacrifice is the wrong message. ______
8. Sunday school is no longer the cornerstone of Christian education. ______
9. Church membership is unimportant. ______
10. Jesus does not call you to preserve a heritage. ______
11. More volunteers to fill all the vacancies will not help rescue the church. ______
12. Dutiful service to a church office is a detour on the journey of life. ______
13. Adding professional staff accelerates church decline. ______
14. It is *not* the pastor's job to visit the hospitals. ______

15. Bible study in the church parlor is futile. ______
16. If you want action, *never* form a committee. ______
17. Actions no longer speak louder than words. ______
18. Mission units do not need to report to church boards. ______
19. Debt freedom always leads to church decline. ______
20. Finance committees should not talk about money. ______
21. Unified budgets artificially limit mission. ______
22. Property maintenance is no longer a measure of faithfulness. ______
23. Strategic planning is overrated. ______
24. Building for eternity makes your church obsolete. ______
25. The best leaders make the most mistakes. ______
26. Church *insiders* are the least able to discern future mission. ______
27. Denominational certification has nothing to do with spiritual leadership. ______
28. Sound theology lacks Christian integrity. ______
29. If you can say it all in words, you've missed the point. ______
30. North America is the *least* Christian continent in the world today. ______

Top 30 Positive Discoveries

Compare the positive discovery that corresponds by number with these shocking insights.

1. **Transformed adults (ages 18-40) are the future of your church.**
   Adults who are changed, gifted, called, and equipped will take care of the children—and everything else!

2. **Everybody wants to be touched by the healing and transforming power of God.**
   The public is desperate to be changed, different, and liberated from their hurts and addictions.

3. **Thriving, growing churches provide multiple opportunities for safe, healthy intimacy.**
   People want to go beyond the coffee urn to bare their souls with a deeply trusted few.

4. **Worship that works is the only spiritual standard in the post-Christendom world.**
   "Good" worship helps people experience the power of God and walk with Jesus—everything else is tactics.

5. **Most people like contemporary music with a strong melody and lots of rhythm.**
   Percussion, guitar, creative instrumentations, and small group ensembles get people's attention.

6. **What matters most is how people feel following the worship service.**
   People want to "feel alive" for worship, and be motivated to learn and serve through the week.

7. **Self-affirmation is the right message.**
   People seeking self-worth give generously to express and celebrate their inner value.

8. **Small groups are the cornerstones of Christian education.**
   Groups in any configuration, meeting during the week in homes, promote Christian growth.

9. **Participation in any aspect of congregational life and mission is everything.**
   Doing hands-on mission, and involvement in ministry are more meaningful than merely belonging to the church.

10. **Jesus calls you to risk everything for mission.**
    If the past helps you grow Christians for the future, use it. If not, the gospel is all that matters.

11. **Core disciples, who in turn make more disciples, expand God's realm.**
    A few people who are ready to go, grow, and mentor are more effective than numerous committees.

12. **Excited pursuit of a call brings personal fulfillment.**
    People would rather fulfill their destiny than spend their time implementing someone else's agenda.

13. **Nurturing amateurs to lead ministries from within the congregation grows the church.**
    The only reason you add staff is to release more gifted, called, and equipped volunteers.

14. **It is the pastoral leader's job to train gifted laity in pastoral care.**
    Clergy are trainers, motivators, and visionaries who equip others to do ministries.

15. **On-the-job, biblical action and reflection bear fruit.**
    Study the Bible in the physical context of work or mission, and reflect on your daily living.

16. **If you want action, find a gifted and called individual and turn them loose.**
    Trained laity, who are free to take initiative, will find whatever help they need.

17. **You must share your faith motivation for every beneficial service.**
    Evangelism and social action are two sides of the same coin.

18. **Mission units must connect weekly with a worship experience.**
    Today's entrepreneurial teams do not need to get permission, but they do need to grow spiritually in worship.

19. **Sound debt management is the key to thriving church development.**
    People today are unafraid of debt, provided it is mission oriented and wisely managed.

20. **Finance committees should talk about deploying servants.**
    Property and money are resources to be used when deploying people for mission.

21. **Capital pools to seed creative ministries multiply mission.**
    Empowered teams take responsibility to raise, manage, and spend the money they need for mission.

22. **Faithfulness is measured by upgradable technologies.**
    Technology is the way people discover and interpret meaning in life; upgrade and grow your church at the same time.

23. **Anticipation of the unpredictable is the art of a thriving church life.**
Spontaneity, flexibility, and planned stress management are part of authentic visions.

24. **Marketability, portability, and flexibility make your church responsive to the mission field.**
The church building is just a tactic that can always be adapted to follow or influence the mission field.

25. **Great leaders intentionally learn from experimentation.**
An intentional strategy to learn from experimentation is more important than strategic planning.

26. **People on the fringe of church life are key to discerning the future.**
Biblical visions are most often revealed to those who have been marginalized.

27. **Spiritual leadership speaks out of its own experience of life struggle and spiritual victory.**
Authenticity is more important than either professional skill or ordination.

28. **Clear Christology is the key to integrity in today's pagan world.**
All you need to know is your experience with Jesus, which your community cannot live without.

29. **Motivating visions are always a "Song in the Heart."**
To get the blood of total strangers pounding, motivating visions are best shared without words.

30. **Today the mission field is right outside your back door.**
Most people in North America are confused or ignorant about even the basics of Christian belief.

Adding Up Your Addictions: Counting Your Opportunities

Add your scores in each of the following areas. Higher numbers indicate areas where you will find it difficult to understand or implement change. Lower numbers indicate possible "entry points" for initiating church transformation. *Remember the statements overlap, because from one direction or another, sooner or later, transformation touches the whole church life system.*

Vision and Identity	Statements 1, 3, 10, 26, 29	Average: _______
Worship and Spirituality	Statements 2, 4, 5, 6, 28	Average: _______
Education and Nurture	Statements 7, 8, 12, 15, 28	Average: _______
Outreach and Mission	Statements 17, 18, 19, 23, 30	Average: _______
Organization and Structure	Statements 11, 13, 16, 22, 24	Average: _______
Stewardship and Finance	Statements 7, 20, 21, 22, 24	Average: _______
Leadership and Membership	Statements 9, 13, 14, 25, 27	Average: _______

THE CHURCH STRESS TEST

FOR CONGREGATIONAL WORSHIP SERVICES

An addiction is an unhealthy behavior pattern that we may deny but truly undermines our health and blocks productive living. Organizations, like individuals, can have such unhealthy behavior patterns. When these addictions are pointed out to us, our stress level increases sharply. The following statements sound extreme, but they contain shocking truths that thriving, growing, vital congregations have discovered.

Let's see where this congregation will feel the most stress in future change. After each statement, identify your personal level of anxiety by assigning a number between 1 and 10. Responses will be gathered during or after two consecutive worship services then averaged. These results will be combined with the other information being collected in the congregational mission assessment tool. Look on the next page to see the *positive* insights of growing churches!

No Anxiety *1 2 3 4 5 6 7 8 9 10* **High Anxiety**

1. The youth are *not* the future of your church. ______
2. Nobody cares about the *mere* presence of God. ______
3. Every dying church in North America is a friendly congregation. ______
4. There is no such thing as "good" worship. ______
5. Most people don't like organ music. ______
6. It doesn't matter what people retain following the worship service. ______
7. Self-sacrifice is the wrong message. ______
8. Sunday school is no longer the cornerstone of Christian education. ______
9. Church membership is unimportant. ______
10. Jesus does not call you to preserve a heritage. ______
11. More volunteers to fill all the vacancies will not help rescue the church. ______
12. Dutiful service to a church office is a detour on the journey of life. ______
13. Adding professional staff accelerates church decline. ______
14. It is *not* the pastor's job to visit the hospitals. ______

15. Bible study in the church parlor is futile. ______
16. If you want action, *never* form a committee. ______
17. Actions no longer speak louder than words. ______
18. Mission units do not need to report to church boards. ______
19. Debt freedom always leads to church decline. ______
20. Finance committees should not talk about money. ______
21. Unified budgets artificially limit mission. ______
22. Property maintenance is no longer a measure of faithfulness. ______
23. Strategic planning is overrated. ______
24. Building for eternity makes your church obsolete. ______
25. The best leaders make the most mistakes. ______
26. Church *insiders* are the least able to discern future mission. ______
27. Denominational certification has nothing to do with spiritual leadership. ______
28. Sound theology lacks Christian integrity. ______
29. If you can say it all in words, you've missed the point. ______
30. North America is the *least* Christian continent in the world today. ______

Top 30 Positive Discoveries

Compare the positive discovery that corresponds by number with these shocking insights.

1. **Transformed adults (ages 18-40) are the future of your church.**
   Adults who are changed, gifted, called, and equipped will take care of the children—and everything else!

2. **Everybody wants to be touched by the healing and transforming power of God.**
   The public is desperate to be changed, different, and liberated from their hurts and addictions.

3. **Thriving, growing churches provide multiple opportunities for safe, healthy intimacy.**
   People want to go beyond the coffee urn to bare their souls with a deeply trusted few.

4. **Worship that works is the only spiritual standard in the post-Christendom world.**
   "Good" worship helps people experience the power of God and walk with Jesus—everything else is tactics.

5. **Most people like contemporary music with a strong melody and lots of rhythm.**
   Percussion, guitar, creative instrumentations, and small group ensembles get people's attention.

6. **What matters most is how people feel following the worship service.**
   People want to "feel alive" for worship and be motivated to learn and serve through the week.

7. **Self-affirmation is the right message.**
   People seeking self-worth give generously to express and celebrate their inner value.

8. **Small groups are the cornerstones of Christian education.**
Groups in any configuration, meeting during the week in homes, promote Christian growth.

9. **Participation in any aspect of congregational life and mission is everything.**
Doing hands-on mission and involvement in ministry is more meaningful than merely belonging to the church.

10. **Jesus calls you to risk everything for mission.**
If the past helps you grow Christians for the future, use it. If not, the gospel is all that matters.

11. **Core disciples, who in turn make more disciples, expand God's realm.**
A few people who are ready to go, grow, and mentor are more effective than numerous committees.

12. **Excited pursuit of a call brings personal fulfillment.**
People would rather fulfill their destiny than spend their time implementing someone else's agenda.

13. **Nurturing amateurs to lead ministries from within the congregation grows the church.**
The only reason you add staff is to release more gifted, called, and equipped volunteers.

14. **It is the pastoral leader's job to train gifted laity in pastoral care.**
Clergy are trainers, motivators, and visionaries who equip others to do ministries.

15. **On-the-job, biblical action and reflection bear fruit.**
Study the Bible in the physical context of work or mission, and reflect on your daily living.

16. **If you want action, find a gifted and called individual and turn them loose.**
Trained laity, who are free to take initiative, will find whatever help they need.

17. **You must share your faith motivation for every beneficial service.**
Evangelism and social action are two sides of the same coin.

18. **Mission units must connect weekly with a worship experience.**
Today's entrepreneurial teams do not need to get permission, but they do need to grow spiritually in worship.

19. **Sound debt management is the key to thriving church development.**
People today are unafraid of debt, provided it is mission oriented and managed wisely.

20. **Finance committees talk about deploying servants.**
Property and money are resources to be used in deploying people for mission.

21. **Capital pools to seed creative ministries multiply mission.**
Empowered teams take responsibility to raise, manage, and spend the money they need for mission.

22. **Faithfulness is measured by upgradable technologies.**
Technology is the way people discover and interpret meaning in life; upgrade and grow your church at the same time.

23. **Anticipation of the unpredictable is the art of a thriving church life.**
Spontaneity, flexibility, and planned stress management are part of authentic visions.

24. **Marketability, portability, and flexibility make your church responsive to the mission field.**
The church building is just a tactic that can always be adapted to follow or influence the mission field.

25. **Great leaders intentionally learn from experimentation.**
An intentional strategy to learn from experimentation is more important than strategic planning.

26. **People on the fringe of church life are key to discerning the future.**
Biblical visions are most often revealed to those who have been marginalized.

27. **Spiritual leadership speaks out of its own experience of life struggle and spiritual victory.**
Authenticity is more important than either professional skill or ordination.

28. **Clear Christology is the key to integrity in today's pagan world.**
All you need to know is your experience with Jesus, which your community cannot live without.

29. **Motivating visions are always a "Song in the Heart."**
To get the blood of total strangers pounding, motivating visions are best shared without words.

30. **Today the mission field is right outside your back door.**
Most people in North America are confused or ignorant about even the basics of Christian belief.

Thank you for allowing us to challenge your thinking!

AN ANCIENT DIAGNOSIS FOR TODAY'S CONGREGATION

As early as the third and fourth centuries after the birth of Christ, Christian leaders had begun to simplify the dread of sin and the hope of grace into basic principles that could easily be applied to daily living. These principles are another example of how premodern thinking can powerfully influence postmodern living.

- The Seven Deadly Sins
- The Seven Cardinal Virtues
- The Seven Acts of Mercy
- The Seven Experiences of Grace

Whatever the intricacies of various creeds, theologies, and belief systems might be, these basic principles are understood and applied self-critically by all Christians. These principles are not about how you think, but about how you behave.

These premodern principles correspond directly with postmodern sensitivity to *addiction, health, service,* and *joy.* These four lifestyle issues are the real keys to inspiring interest in Christian faith among unchurched people—in either the previous or the current "apostolic age." Pure dogma and systematic theology, or political correctness and social ideology, will not do it. These lifestyle-oriented principles for abundant living will do it.

- *Addiction* (Seven Deadly Sins) is a habitual, self-destructive behavior pattern that people chronically deny, but which rob life of meaning and vitality. The seven deadly sins are: pride, covetousness, lust, envy, anger, gluttony, and sloth.

- *Health* (Seven Cardinal Virtues) is only fully, and holistically experienced when addiction is overcome through seven cardinal virtues: faith, charity, prudence, hope, justice, temperance, and fortitude.

- *Service* (Seven Acts of Mercy) is the outward vehicle of self-fulfillment through which healthy people extend the benefits of life to others: feeding the hungry, giving drink to the thirsty, clothing the naked, visiting the sick, housing the homeless, rescuing the captives, and honoring the dead.

- *Joy* (Seven Experiences of Grace) is the inward vehicle of self-fulfillment through which healthy people receive the benefits of life through the intervention of a higher power. Christendom has identified these with seven sacraments, which I describe more broadly as: rebirth (baptism), covenant (confirmation), repentance (penance), communion, loyal intimacy (marriage), calling (ordination), and acceptance (unction).

For ordinary Christians, the power of the Reformation was not its doctrinal critique of Catholic dogma, nor even its biblical interpretation; rather it was the Reformation's clear confrontation of the seven addictive forces that were destroying life's meaning and vitality. The ninety-five theses of Luther and the church dogmatics of Calvin were significant for scholars, but it was the graphic images of personified ecclesiastical covetousness carrying off a bag of plunder or ecclesiastical anger beating a woman or ecclesiastical pride riding a warhorse that fired the indignation of ordinary people.

The same principles that are applied to individual lifestyles can be applied to organizational lifestyles. This is a confrontation with *corporate addictions*. Those who have read my book *Kicking Habits: Welcome Relief for Addicted Churches* know that I have long believed overcoming addictions is the most fundamental challenge for church renewal. One must look beyond the mere introduction of new *programs* in the church and transform the entire *system* of church life.

- ❑ For the addicted individual, the mere introduction of a self-help book, diet technique, or chemical will not ultimately solve the problem. One must change the flow of life physically, psychologically, socially, and spiritually.

- ❑ For the addicted church organization, the mere introduction of a paved parking lot, magnetic youth minister, or improved sound system will not ultimately solve the problem of church decline. One must change the whole flow of life as newcomers and participants experience the church.

Addiction subtly enslaves everything the church does in every committee, program, activity, and leadership position. It profoundly warps the organization's ability to perceive the truth about the organization and God's purpose in the world. It ultimately sabotages the best-laid strategic plan and the most sincere efforts of committed church leaders. What happened to that wonderful mission statement? Why didn't that new worship service attract newcomers? Why do we have a great preacher but continue to have chronic operating deficits each fall? Why do our lay leaders keep burning out and our staff keep disappearing to disability? Addictions.

This conviction about the power of addiction has led me to customize my congregational consultation tool to address all eleven subsystems of congregational life so that it not only identifies strengths and weaknesses, but it also traces hidden corporate addictions throughout the entire congregational life. I use the Seven Deadly Sins and the Seven Cardinal Virtues to symbolically measure the health of the church. Admittedly, this is my own extrapolation of these historic principles for the practical purposes of church consultation, and these two groups of seven principles do not always link tidily together. I hope church historians and systematic theologians will accept my apologies for its inaccuracies—and I am sure they can offer suggestions to refine the tool. Nonetheless, it can help you gain insight into the *real, systemic issues* that hold your church back from abundant life and effective mission.

Each question in the master summary of the assessment tool is coded to identify it with one of the addiction-health polarities below. The middle column indicates which questions pertain to which addiction-health polarity. This allows you to focus on a particular set of questions to determine the degree of addiction or health that is experienced by that church. This is not a quantifiable science. It is an art. Study the definitions below and anticipate how you might "score" your church on a scale of 1 (deeply addicted) to 10 (extremely healthy). Later, when your research is complete, ask several church leaders to do this also and compare your results. If a professional church consultant has interpreted the assessment tool, compare his or her assessment as well.

The Seven Deadly Sins		The Seven Cardinal Virtues
1. PRIDE: The elevation of the church to ultimacy. Institutional arrogance. Self-centeredness that expects the world to accommodate itself to the forms, habits, and expectations of institutional religion. It is the belief that the world revolves around the church, must wait for the church, and is ultimately judged by the church. It is the egotistical conviction that the mission field can be addressed at the convenience of the church.	**PF Questions** 1, 2, 3, 4, 7, 12, 15, 22, 23, 30, 31, 32, 37, 38, 49, 52, 53, 57, 77, 84, 90, 92, 102, 104, 109, 110	**1. FAITH** The surrender of the church to the ultimacy of Christ. Institutional humility. The compassionate prioritizing of strategies that lead the church to adapt itself to the cultural forms of real people. It is the urgency to engage in mission now, before it is too late, and before God judges the church for failing to rescue the lost. It is the selfless conviction that the mission of the church is more important than the survival of an institutional franchise.
2. COVETOUSNESS The institutional desire to possess what is not theirs. An obsession with material wealth. The elevation of "things" to a core value. It is the preoccupation of the church with property and money, and the desire to acquire the wealth of others to perpetuate institutional comfort. It is the habitual reduction of programs to balance the budget, obsession with debt freedom, and the expectation that society should spend itself for the sake of denominational heritage.	**CC Questions** 1, 7, 8, 27, 28, 33, 38, 44, 64, 66, 67, 70, 71, 73, 74, 75, 78, 83, 85, 86, 91, 92, 95, 97, 100, 101, 106, 107, 110	**2. CHARITY** The institutional audacity to give away life. The acquisition of wealth for the sole purpose of maximizing mission. The motivation to walk a second mile, endure abuse, and give away the best. The habitual, positive preference to *give* a break rather than *get* a tax break. It is the recognition by the church that stewardship embraces everything and there is no separation between sacred and secular. It is the readiness to risk property, modify plans, and change agendas to seize moments to bless others.
3. LUST Abuse of others as a means to personal or corporate satisfaction. An absolute desire to control others completely. It is the passion to possess the life of another or make another dependent upon the organization or its leaders. It is *eros* disguised as *agape*, or ego camouflaged as pastoral care. It is the demand to be praised, loved, and cared for.	**LP Questions** 9, 13, 14, 17, 19, 21, 22, 23, 39, 40, 43, 54, 61, 63, 69, 70, 76, 77, 81, 82, 83, 85, 86, 87, 91, 92, 98, 99, 103, 105, 108, 110	**3. PRUDENCE** Respect for another's intrinsic autonomy and worth. Wisdom that limits self-satisfaction for the sake of another. Responsible freedom. It is the readiness to give permission to act independently and discover self-fulfillment beyond institutional commitments. It is the true unity of *eros* and *agape*, or the balance of self-sacrifice and self-affirmation.
4. ENVY The desire to be something other than what God created the organization to be. Self-rejection. The refusal to acknowledge one's own mission potential and the jealous imitation of another organization's lifestyle. It is blaming other powers for organizational failure. It is habitual lamentation that "if someone or something were different, we would be all right."	**EH Questions** 1, 5, 6, 27, 28, 33, 36, 38, 41, 44, 50, 52, 57, 58, 73, 78, 80, 92, 93, 94, 96, 102, 104, 109, 110	**4. HOPE** The desire to become whatever God wills. Self-acceptance. The conviction that God's power will bear fruit and that the church can overcome all obstacles when it is true to its unique calling. It is taking ownership of failure, and intentionally learning from inevitable mistakes. It is the habitual celebration and belief that "if we hold Jesus' hand, we can walk on water."
5. GLUTTONY Consumption. Excess, Self-aggrandizement. It is the desire to bring people in, rather than send people out. It is preoccupation with how newcomers can serve the institution rather than serve God. It is valuing size over quality, accountability over productivity, and process over results. It is the willingness to waste energy in pointless pursuits.	**GT Questions** 11, 12, 16, 19, 20, 23, 24, 25, 29, 31, 34, 35, 40, 48, 49, 54, 60, 65, 68, 71, 81, 92, 93, 94, 96, 97, 108, 110	**5. TEMPERANCE** Moderation. Reasonable limitation. Self-control. It is the desire to bring people into church so they can more effectively live beyond the church. It is the appropriate fulfillment of needs, building up of character, and training of relevant skills. It is valuing excellence over mediocrity, trust over control. It is the willingness to spend everything for a truly greater good.
6. ANGER The desire to harm or hurt. Physical, emotional, relational, or spiritual violence. It is the habitual, negative preference to kill, repulse, or limit the good within others. It is sardonic pleasure in justice and twisted joy in retribution. It is misrepresenting prophetic leadership by taking delight in breaking relationships, splitting organizations, or humiliating adversaries.	**AJ Questions** 1, 5, 6, 26, 38, 39, 45, 50, 55, 64, 66, 67, 71, 75, 78, 79, 92, 95, 98, 99, 101, 106, 107, 110	**6. JUSTICE** The desire to vindicate and redeem. Physical, emotional, relational, or spiritual healing. It is principled counteraction against violent people. It is redemptive punishment for the goal of reconciliation. It is unbearable restlessness in the face of inequality, bigotry, or cultural insensitivity. It is visionary leadership that delights in synthesizing "both-and" situations. It is the difference between victory and peace.
7. SLOTH Laziness. Lack of discipline. It is the expectation that others (staff or volunteers) will do your work for you. It is the profound unwillingness to grow personally, spiritually, or professionally. It is the easy readiness to give up. It is the despairing conviction of organizational impotence that paralyzes action.	**SF Questions** 8, 10, 13, 14, 18, 23, 24, 25, 30, 32, 33, 34, 35, 42, 45, 46, 47, 48, 51, 53, 56, 59, 60, 62, 68, 72, 80, 88, 89, 92, 101, 110	**7. FORTITUDE** Energy. Discipline. It is the ability to do whatever it takes to discern, address, and accomplish one's own work. It is a passion to grow in every way. It is dogged persistence to try every means to accomplish goals. It is courageous confidence to tap hidden resources in order to take mission risks.

The Seven Acts of Mercy measure the degree to which the congregation fulfills itself through outward, beneficial service. Consider the list of various missions and ministries (as identified in question 71 of the assessment tool) of congregational members, congregational groups, and the congregation as a whole. Place each one in the context of one of the acts of mercy described below.

1. *Feeding the hungry:* The ways in which the congregation addresses the physical needs of the world through food gifts, coaching for self-reliance, and environmental protection.

    1.

    2.

    3.

2. *Providing drink for the thirsty:* The ways in which the congregation helps people learn, grow, and satisfy their yearning for knowledge, quality relationships, and deep spirituality.

    1.

    2.

    3.

3. *Clothing the naked:* The ways in which the congregation protects the abused or the vulnerable, and equips the lowly to build self-esteem.

    1.

    2.

    3.

4. *Visiting the sick:* The ways in which the congregation supports both church insiders and church outsiders who are sick in body, mind, or heart.

    1.

    2.

    3.

5. *Housing the homeless:* The ways in which the congregation welcomes strangers into the church or community and coaches them to safely, joyfully, and responsibly live in a different place.

    1.

    2.

    3.

6. *Rescuing the captives:* The ways in which the congregation invests money and energy to rescue those who are trapped by bigotry, poverty, or politics.

    1.

    2.

    3.

7. *Honoring the dead:* The ways in which the congregation helps people confront death and dying with dignity and hope.

    1.

    2.

    3.

Now refer to the chart from question 71 again to discover how church members actually participate in these acts of mercy. Are they only deploying property? Are they only raising money? Are they helping set policy and direction for the mission? Are they involved personally? Who is involved—volunteers or staff?

Mission or Ministry	**Property use only (free use or rental)**	**Financial support only**	**Church members set policy**	**Church members participate hands-on in the mission**	**Approximate # of church members involved**	**# of staff or church leaders involved**

The diagnosis of church health does not just depend upon the *quantity* of ministries done in each category, but also the *quality* of missions. Congregations committed only to rentals and fund-raising, for example, are not as healthy as those with church members shaping mission policy or participating in hands-on mission. Relative commitment to these acts of mercy is a clue to the health of the congregation and also a remedy through which the congregation can overcome addiction.

Finally, the Seven Experiences of Grace measure the degree to which the congregation experiences joy through the inward intervention of God. This should by no means be limited to liturgy or worship. In church consultation, the experience of grace is revealed through the storytelling of congregational participants and the clarity and enthusiasm of their congregational identity for their values, beliefs, vision, and mission. The more spontaneous congregational participants are in celebrating and articulating their experiences of grace, the healthier the congregation is. The more daring and intentional congregational participants are in living out their values and beliefs, the healthier the congregation is. The more diverse such experiences of grace become, the healthier the congregation is.

1. *Rebirth:* The ways congregational participants experience and celebrate personal transformations in relationship to Christ.

2. *Covenant:* The ways congregational participants experience being chosen by God and mold their lifestyles around Christ.

3. *Repentance:* The ways congregational participants accept criticism and reprioritize their time and energy in obedience to Christ.

4. *Communion:* The ways congregational participants experience union with God in a daily walk with Jesus.

5. *Loyal Intimacy:* The ways congregational participants prioritize and celebrate fidelity in marriage, family, friendship, or any intentionally covenanted relationship in Christ.

6. *Calling:* The ways congregational participants discover their destiny in God's plan and accompany Christ into the mission field.

7. *Acceptance:* The ways congregational participants receive ultimate acceptance of all that they are and look forward, with hope, to eternity.

These experiences of grace are truly sacramental in the sense that they represent the intersection of divine ministry and human life that is initiated by God for the redemption of human beings.

Once again let me say that the discernment of addiction or health is more an art than a science. People who are outside the immediate congregational environment usually have the clearest discernment—just as people outside an addictive relationship usually identify addiction more easily. A veteran consultant can bring a wealth of experience from different churches to bear on this assessment. A denominational consultant, leaders from other congregations beyond the community, or other observers may also be able to discern relative addiction or health better. Test your interpretation of the facts and experiences of the church with others.

The postmodern world is filled with "origin-al" thinkers. People invent new ways to reflect on life and act in mission. Yet at the same time, people return to original, ancient wisdom to inspire and guide their contemporary thinking. When it comes to addressing the corporate addictions of the church, look to the ancients for assistance.

INSTALLATION INSTRUCTIONS

Installation Instructions for *Facing Reality: A Congregational Mission Assessment Tool,* CD-ROM Edition

Note: If the Adobe Acrobat Reader 3.0 or 4.0 is already installed on your system, skip to Step 2 ("Installing *Facing Reality: A Congregational Mission Assessment Tool,* CD-ROM Edition") below.

Step 1: Installing the Adobe Acrobat Reader 3.0

You have the choice to install to your fixed disk either the Acrobat Reader 3.0 or the Acrobat Reader Plus Search 3.0.

In Windows 3.x, from Program Manager or File Manager, select FILE/RUN. Using the drive letter of your CD-ROM drive, type the following (the examples below assume that "D" is the drive letter of your CD-ROM drive):

D:ACROREAD\WIN\RDR_SRCH\16BIT\SETUP.EXE

In Windows 95, 98, ME, or 2000, select RUN from the START menu and type the following:

D:\ACROREAD\WIN\RDR_SRCH\32BIT\SETUP.EXE

If you wish to conserve hard drive space, you may load only Adobe Acrobat Reader 3.0 (and not Adobe Acrobat Reader Plus Search 3.0) to your fixed disk. To do so, follow the steps above, substituting the following file:

Windows 3.x: D:\AR16E30.EXE

Windows 95, 98, ME, or 2000: D:\AR32E30.EXE

For more information on installation, open the file D:\README.TXT.

In Macintosh System 7.0 or higher, click on ACROREAD\MAC\READER+SEARCH\READER\Install Acrobat Reader 3.0.

For more information on installation, open the file README_M.MAC.

Step 2:
Installing *Facing Reality: A Congregational Mission Assessment Tool,* CD-ROM Edition

After you have installed Adobe Acrobat 3.0 (or if the Adobe Acrobat Reader 3.0 or 4.0 is already installed on your system), follow the following steps:

A. Open the Acrobat Reader by clicking on the Acrobat Reader icon in the Adobe Acrobat program group.

B. Select FILE/OPEN from the menu.

C. From the Open Dialog, select one of the three following files (depending on which part of the book you wish to see):

D:\FCGRLTY1.PDF (containing pages 1 through 40 of *Facing Reality*).

D:\FCGRLTY2.PDF (containing pages 41 through 73 of *Facing Reality*).

D:\FCGRLTY3.PDF (containing pages 74 through 110 of *Facing Reality*).

D. *Facing Reality: A Congregational Mission Assessment Tool,* CD-ROM Edition, allows you to fill in the many forms and questionnaires of the Congregational Mission Assessment Tool on screen, and output them to a printer. **PLEASE NOTE:** The Adobe Acrobat Reader 3.0 will not allow you to save your work to disk, so we suggest that you print each page as it is completed.

NOTE: If you have not used the Adobe Acrobat Reader 3.0 before, or if you have questions about its operation, refer to the online help available from the HELP function on the menu. You can reach Abingdon Software Technical Support by calling (615) 749-6777, or by posting a message on the Abingdon Software Support Forum at http://www.abingdon.org/soft_frm.htm.